METHODS AND STYLES IN THE STUDY OF CULTURE

CHANDLER & SHARP PUBLICATIONS IN ANTHROPOLOGY

GENERAL EDITORS: L. L. Langness and Robert B. Edgerton

ROBERT B. EDGERTON
AND
L. L. LANGNESS

UNIVERSITY OF CALIFORNIA

LOS ANGELES

Chandler & Sharp Publishers, Inc.

11A COMMERCIAL BOULEVARD, NOVATO, CA 94947

COPYRIGHT © 1974 BY CHANDLER & SHARP PUBLISHERS, INC.
ALL RIGHTS RESERVED
LIBRARY OF CONGRESS CATALOG CARD NUMBER 74-89
INTERNATIONAL STANDARD BOOK NUMBER 0-88316-508-2
PRINTED IN THE UNITED STATES OF AMERICA

Library of Congress Cataloging in Publication Data

Edgerton, Robert B.   1931-
    Methods and styles in the study of culture.

    (Chandler & Sharp publications in anthropology)
    Bibliography: p.
    1. Ethnology--Methodology.   I.   Langness, Lewis L.,
joint author.   II.   Title.
GN345.E35   301.2'01'8   74-89
ISBN 0-88316-508-2

THIRD PRINTING, 1979

To Better Understanding among All People

CONTENTS

ILLUSTRATIONS

PREFACE

Human beings appear always to have had an intense fascination with the world around them, with plants and animals, birds, the sea, mountains, plains, and the heavens. This fascination is evidenced by the oldest examples of art we know —cave paintings and *petroglyphs*, sculptures and carvings, and even the most ancient myths and stories that have survived. Most of all, human beings seem to have been fascinated and entranced with other human beings. Anthropology is the scientific expression of man's curiosity about his living—not only about how other people have lived in other places and at other times, but also about how we live here and now. Many of the people with whom anthropologists have worked appear to be remarkably different and "exotic"; others do not seem to be very different at all. But there is always a clear and compelling underlying common humanity even in those who appear to be most different. The repeated personal discovery of this truth has made anthropologists treat the fieldwork experience with much respect. This book is about the anthropological experience—how anthropologists try to understand the lives of other people. It also explores how they think and write about man's common humanity so that others may come to share in their knowledge and understanding.

We have written this book primarily for beginning students in anthropology —whether they intend to continue their study of anthropology or go into other fields does not matter. We do not intend it to be a completely thorough and detailed exposition of the methods used by anthropologists. Instead, it is a broad overview which gives the reader a sufficient acquaintance with the methods of gathering ethnographic information, the styles of presenting it, and the techniques of analyzing it so that anthropology and the range of anthropological writings will be more familiar, more understandable, more meaningful, and more enjoyable. For those who wish to pursue the methods, styles, and analyses of anthropologists in more detail or at greater length, selected references for each section have been provided.

Anthropological methods, when compared with the methods of the physical sciences or even with the methods of other social sciences, do not seem very sophisticated or complex. Although cultural anthropologists do use computers, motion pictures, tape recorders, videotape, and other technological devices, they have no specialized machinery or gadgets such as the electron microscope or the atom smasher. They have no methods or techniques that are mysterious or particularly difficult to comprehend. Many of their methods have been borrowed from other disciplines. Much of what they do is also done by others. But even so, no social-science methods have quite the mystique of anthropological fieldwork, nor do most of them involve the same amount of emotional involvement or generate the same amount of criticism. The anthropological fieldwork experience is a unique and valuable way of understanding other cultures. Although a precise appreciation of this experience is difficult to convey, some understanding of it is surely a requisite for an appreciation of the field of cultural anthropology.

The discussion of anthropological methods in this book has been divided into three parts. Part I discusses the nature and process of fieldwork, including the various techniques anthropologists use in their field research. Part II deals with the styles anthropologists and others have used to organize and write about these data for presentation to other anthropologists and to the public, as well as their motives and purposes in doing so. This area of styles is much neglected in anthropology but must be understood if one is to appreciate the difference between anthropology as a science and anthropology as part of the humanities, between writing ethnography and writing ethnographic fiction, and between professional anthropology and other attempts to comprehend and portray the human condition.

Finally, in Part III, the book reviews the ways in which anthropologists analyze and attempt to explain and compare the findings of fieldwork in their effort to discover or verify generalizations about human behavior and culture. It will be seen that, for anthropologists, the scientific search for laws rests most fundamentally upon the skill with which fieldwork is done and the ways in which the findings of fieldwork are presented. It might be argued that the resulting anthropological explanations are often at a simple level, that they do not compare with explanations in the so-called "hard sciences" such as physics or chemistry. Indeed, anthropologists and other social scientists are a long way from the accuracy and predictability of physics or chemistry; but human behavior itself, in its enormous variation and complexity, is a long way from the subject matter of physics or chemistry. Furthermore, in terms of its brief history, and more especially in terms of the limited resources that have been made available to it, anthropology is still in its infancy when compared with physics and chemistry. Its potential both as a science and as a humanity is great.

Anthropology is the study of "man and his works"—of all of us and of what we do. It enables us to go beyond our own experience toward an understanding of how people live in very different parts of the world. By understanding others we hope to better understand ourselves and to bring closer a true brotherhood of mankind. How anthropologists learn about other peoples and how they write about them is of singular importance for all of us.

R. B. E.
L. L. L.

ACKNOWLEDGMENTS

We are grateful to many people for their help with this book. Most specifically, we owe our thanks to George Guilmet, Gilbert Herdt, Jill Korbin, Paul Preuss, and Thomas S. Weisner for their comments on one or another version of the manuscript, to Jae Stewart for typing its many versions, to Joany Langness for skillful proofreading and indexing, and to Cecile Edgerton for helping to write it from start to finish. We appreciate support provided by PHS Grant HD-04612-05, the Mental Retardation Research Center, UCLA.

R. B. E.
L. L. L.

METHODS AND STYLES IN THE STUDY OF CULTURE

PART I THE METHODS OF ANTHROPOLOGICAL FIELDWORK

This book is about how anthropologists study culture. But before we begin our discussion of methods and styles in the study of culture we should consider what culture is and why anthropologists study it. *Culture* refers to a people's way of life. Everywhere that people live on earth, they follow customary ways of behaving — of eating, hunting, expressing affection, raising children, reacting to death, and the like. Culture is expressed by these patterns of behavior; the patterns reflect the codes or rules that guide how people behave — how they speak, make love, wage war, greet strangers, or whatever else it is they do. Everywhere, these patterns and the codes behind them give human existence its regularity, purpose, and meaning. Man creates culture, and he passes it on to his children; but in the same way, culture shapes man. Human beings behave and think and feel in a cultural world, and each group of people lives in a somewhat different cultural world. To understand mankind it is necessary to understand these different cultures and how they have come about. This is the task anthropologists have set for themselves.

We shall concentrate in this book upon the methods employed by anthropologists in understanding culture, the styles they use to present what they know to others, and the efforts they make to compare cultures in a search for general principles of human behavior.

This first section of the book deals with methods. In anthropology as in any science, the methods employed help to determine what kinds of facts will be gathered; the facts, in turn, lead to the development of theories; and the theories, in their turn, influence methods. We cannot entirely ignore any of these. We will focus almost exclusively on methods here, however, for too often the important role played by methods in this relationship has been ignored.

1

Fieldwork: The Anthropologist's Way of Understanding

The birth of anthropology as a discipline took place in an age which believed strongly in the idea of "progress." Evolutionary theory played the part of midwife. The early days of anthropology were marked by much speculation about the presumed evolutionary course of culture and the reasons for the cultural differences which existed between societies. This was mostly "armchair" theorizing; few of the theorists had firsthand knowledge of other peoples. Far too much reliance was placed on the accounts, frequently biased and distorted, of early travelers, journalists, and missionaries. Thus it soon became apparent that if anthropologists were to get their feet on solid theoretical ground, they needed a method whereby they could obtain complete and accurate descriptions of cultures in every part of the world.

Fieldwork, a prolonged personal study in which the anthropologist resides within the society he is attempting to describe, was the method anthropology was looking for. Franz Boas, frequently called the "father" of modern anthropology, is often credited with having started the procedures that finally became formalized in the closing years of the nineteenth century as "fieldwork."

Boas conducted his first fieldwork among the Eskimo of Baffin Island in 1883, and though he was originally trained in Germany as a physicist, he used no scientific instruments or experiments in his attempts to understand and describe Eskimo culture. The only instrument needed was the human one that decoded the cultural patterns and found the humanity beneath them.

Boas wrote:

After long and intimate intercourse with the Eskimo, it was with feelings of sorrow and regret that I parted from my Arctic friends. I had seen that they enjoyed life, as we do; that nature is also beautiful to them; that feelings of friendship also root in the Eskimo heart; that, although the character of their life is so rude as compared to civilized life, the Eskimo is a man as we are; his feelings, his virtues and his shortcomings are based on human nature like ours. (quoted in Hays, 1958:234-235)

The process of fieldwork had given Boas firsthand and important information about Eskimo culture, but it had also given him insight into the basic human nature shared by all men, even "primitives," a point by no means understood or believed by many educated men in the 1880's. What gave force and authority to Boas's opinions was the method by which these opinions were formed. They grew out of fieldwork—direct, person-to-person involvement in the lives of so-called "primitive" people. In the years that followed, other important principles about the nature of man and the nature of culture began to come out of fieldwork and provided much of the foundation upon which modern cultural anthropology has been based.

Fieldwork is not just a single method but a varied set of procedures. The core of fieldwork is *participant-observation*. As participant-observer, the anthropologist lives intimately as a member of the society he has chosen to study. He shares in the people's day-to-day activities, watches as they eat, fight, and dance, listens to their commonplace and exciting conversations, and slowly begins to live and understand life as they do. But he also remains detached from their life, at least to some degree. He is not living among another people to enjoy their way of life. He is there to understand it and then to report his understanding to others. Complete involvement, then, is incompatible with the anthropologist's primary goals, but complete detachment is incompatible with fieldwork. Successful fieldwork requires a balance between the two, a balancing act which is every bit as difficult as it sounds.

The kind of understanding that arises from being a participant-observer takes time. Anthropologists count on spending a substantial period in the field; most go for at least a year if possible, and many stay longer or return for a second visit. In the small societies that anthropologists have typically studied, the natural unit of time is a year. Throughout man's history, nature and the seasons have been closely tied to economic life and through that to man's social rounds. Groups form and disperse, activities change. There are times of hunger and want balanced by times of feasting, celebrating, and plenty. A stay of at least a year is usually required for the anthropologist to acquire an understanding of the range of behaviors and customs in a strange society.

Fieldwork is based upon several important but often implicit principles. The first of these is the belief that the best tool for studying an alien culture and coming to understand it is the intellect, sensitivity, and emotion of another human being. Man is uniquely suited to understand his fellow men and the meaning of life in any other culture. A common thread runs through all of man's cultures, and a human being, given the chance, can learn the cultural patterns of any one of them. Tests and questionnaires given to the members of another culture may provide a researcher with a large fund of information, but in order to interpret the answers and understand what lies behind them, someone must learn and explain the *cultural code*. Anthropologists believe that taking the role of participant-observer in another culture enables them to do this.

A second principle, intimately related to the first, is the conviction that the culture must be seen through the eyes of those who live it in addition to the eyes of the scientific observer. This principle is necessary if Western fieldworkers are to avoid imposing Western standards of thought or feeling upon non-Western man. People's lives must be understood as they themselves understand them, not merely as we as outsiders understand them. One of the greatest of anthropological fieldworkers, Bronislaw Malinowski, helped to set the task: ". . . to grasp the native's point of view, his relation to life, to realize *his* vision of *his* world" (1922:25). Nowadays we refer to this approach as *emic* and contrast it with the *etic* one, the outsider's understanding. To see life as others do requires involvement, participation, and human empathy; otherwise one remains an outsider. Yet there must also be some intellectual detachment, or this hard-won insider's view can never be effectively analyzed or reported.

A final principle, called *holism*, dictates that culture must be seen as a whole. Cultural behaviors must not be isolated from the context in which they occur nor from any other significant cultural aspects to which they are related. Thus fieldwork does not lead simply to the study of religion or economics or child training, but rather to the study of the interrelationship of these and all the other aspects of human life that together form a cultural whole.

This principle of holism is based in part upon an anthropological commitment to naturalistic understanding. *Naturalism* requires that human behavior be viewed in the context in which it naturally occurs (as part of ongoing life in a society rather than as part of an experiment in a laboratory) and that the process of understanding should disturb that behavior as little as possible. Anthropologists doing fieldwork attempt to behave so that their presence has as little influence as possible on the behavior of the people being studied.

In the past, anthropologists have typically chosen small societies in which they can apply the principle of holism to their fieldwork. Such a small society provides a relatively self-contained political and economic unit with few important ties to surrounding societies; the anthropologist is thus able to make a relatively complete study of an entire society. In practice, as might be expected, it is never possible to see the whole of a culture. Fieldwork invariably reflects the interests and opportunities of each anthropologist and varies in the emphasis given to some aspects of culture over others. The guiding principle of holism remains, however, and it provides a powerful perspective for examining human behavior.

The commitment to a naturalistic approach is a commitment to an attempt to discover the truth about another culture. Fieldwork is the anthropologist's attempt to achieve a faithful rendition of another cultural world.

To apply these principles in fieldwork is a formidable task, as the British anthropologist E. E. Evans-Pritchard makes remarkably clear in the following comment (1954:82):

> To succeed [in fieldwork] a man must be able to abandon himself without reserve, and he must also have intuitive powers . . . ability, special training, and love of a careful scholarship . . . the imaginative insight of the artist . . . and the literary skill necessary to translate a foreign culture into the language of one's own. . . . he must have in addition to a wide knowledge of anthropology, a feeling for form and pattern, and a touch of genius.

This is obviously a tall order and even the most self-important of anthropologists would have to admit that evidence of genius is not a requisite for fieldwork. But Evans-Pritchard does make the point intended: fieldwork is difficult and demanding. He might have added that it also is important and rewarding.

We should pause a moment to distinguish anthropological fieldwork from other kinds of experiences that Western men and women have in non-Western societies. In the present day, few areas of the world are any longer beyond the reach of governmental officials, journalists, or packaged tours. But for many years most of the world's societies were visited only by a solitary governmental officer, a missionary, a trader or two, and sometimes an anthropologist. Today, governments have many more representatives, journalists travel everywhere, tourists travel to all parts of the globe, and Peace Corps volunteers spend years in remote villages and towns. All of these people may sometimes suffer from the physical and psychological hazards of life in a world less hygienic, less familiar than their own. But however much their travels and work may demand of them, they do not demand as much as does fieldwork. Government officers go to such places to govern, missionaries to reveal and convert, tourists to experience wonders, Peace Corpsmen to help. Fieldwork demands *understanding* of an alien way of life, and it demands that this understanding be communicated so that it may undergo critical scrutiny by the anthropological community. Not only does the anthropologist face an intimidating intellectual challenge, but he also faces possible disapproval and rejection by his colleagues if his fieldwork does not measure up to difficult standards.

It is little wonder, then, that every anthropologist, whether young or old, wise or foolish, female or male, experienced or not, can encounter not only physical illness during fieldwork but also psychological depression, discomfort, fear, anger, shock, and humiliation. There may also be deep satisfaction, new insight, and lasting friendship. The reasons for these reactions will be clearer as we explain the details of the fieldwork experience.

Margaret Mead, the distinguished American anthropologist, after years of experience that has included fieldwork in eight different cultures, has put it this way: "The wonder to me is not that young anthropologists fail, but that so many succeed" (1970:305).

In the following discussion of methods in anthropology we will follow the course of a typical fieldwork experience: preparation and training, techniques that can be used in the field, and the final return of the anthropologist to his own culture. We hope to provide an understanding of how and why fieldwork is done, for without an understanding of how this unique kind of research is done, it is impossible fully to appreciate or evaluate anthropologists' efforts to provide truthful accounts of other cultures.

Getting Ready to Live in the Field: The Preparation and Training of an Anthropologist

An anthropologist begins to prepare himself for the field experience long before he ever plunges into a strange society in an attempt to understand and describe its culture. It is this preparation, along with his motives, that will make his description of life in another society different from the accounts of explorers, journalists, or missionaries working in foreign lands. What the anthropologist observes and records is based upon years of training in the concepts, theories, and methods of

FIELDWORK IN THE NEW GUINEA HIGHLANDS; LISA FAITHORN. (Courtesy of Harold Levine and Lisa Faithorn)

cultural anthropology. Though he may find adventure living in an exotic society, his purpose is work—work to accomplish his goal—and he counts on the methods and techniques that have grown up in anthropology over the years to enable him to perform this difficult task.

As part of his training, the anthropology student immerses himself in the ethnographic literature that describes other cultures. Although the student may personally be most interested in the cultures of Latin America, he or she reads about how the Eskimo resourcefully exists in the Arctic and how the resilient Aborigines survive in the deserts of Australia, about the social arrangements in a middle-class American suburb, and about the network of kinfolk and friends in a Greek fishing village. In this fashion, he begins to become acquainted with the diversity of human culture. Eventually, the student becomes capable of comparing what he will find in his own fieldwork with what is known from other cultures throughout the world. Similarities and differences will stand out, and possible explanations will come to mind.

While the anthropology student is discovering just how many cultural differences there are in the ways men and women go courting, bring up children, and bury their dead, at the same time he is becoming aware of certain universal features that occur in all societies. The student learns about the inevitable presence of religious beliefs and of social distinctions based on age and sex, about the almost universal existence of the *nuclear family*, about the tendency to clothe important cultural themes in symbolism and myth, about the fact that leadership is almost always in the hands of men, and about many similar things that appear to be found everywhere in human culture. Over the years, the anthropology student develops an understanding of what is universal and what is particular in human cultures, and this knowledge, combined with his understanding of cultural differences, provides a necessary background for fieldwork in any society.

The anthropologist continues throughout his career to add to his fund of information on different societies. This information helps him to understand how cultures change, what conditions may influence a particular practice or belief, which practices tend to put a strain on people who follow them, why certain kinds of social conflict cannot easily be resolved, what kinds of cultural practices are typically found together, and so on. Anthropology is a comparative science. It is by comparing human behavior under various conditions, in all places throughout time, that the anthropologist develops the understanding necessary to do fieldwork.

Learning Anthropological Methods and Concepts

Anthropology, like the rest of the social sciences, is a relatively young discipline; fieldwork as its basic research technique is younger still. It became an important technique in America in the early 1900's under the sponsorship of Franz

Boas, who sent out many young anthropologists such as Margaret Mead, Ruth Benedict, Robert Lowie, and Alfred Kroeber. In Britain, young anthropologists were learning about fieldwork from such prominent anthropologists as A. R. Radcliffe-Brown and Bronislaw Malinowski. These early anthropologists were given little formal direction in how to conduct their fieldwork. Especially in the United States, fieldwork was shaped by the ingenuity and personality of each individual. Each was expected to formulate his or her own field problem and then originate the techniques necessary for solving it.

Many of the prominent anthropologists of today have criticized their professors for sending them to the field with so little formal preparation. Anthropologists have wryly recounted the frustration they felt when they asked their professors for advice about how to conduct their first jobs of fieldwork. The advice they received often consisted solely of instructions to "take a lot of pencils" or to send ahead a large supply of novels to ward off boredom. Even in more recent years some got the same sort of offhand answers to serious, anxious questions; Alan Beals illustrates (1970:38):

> In 1952, on my way to India, I asked a distinguished British anthropologist to tell me his secret of success in doing fieldwork. His response was "Never accept free housing, and always carry a supply of marmalade."

Many anthropologists have referred to this lack of preparation as the "sink-or-swim" philosophy of fieldwork, and have criticized the view of fieldwork as a mystical experience or initiation rite rather than as a scientific procedure. Laura Nader has argued that anthropologists positively value a rough field experience and give prestige to those who suffer the most in fieldwork, as long as they succeed in doing their research (1970:114):

> The student is thrown into the ethnographic ocean, and nature takes its course. If he is worth his salt, he will return from the field an anthropologist.

These criticisms have merit and are generally true, but there is another side to the story as well. Before anthropology's phenomenal growth in the last two decades, it was a small profession in which a great deal of informal discussion served both directly and indirectly to prepare the young fieldworker for the task ahead. Furthermore, as we shall discuss later, there are dangers in being *too* explicit about how to do fieldwork, just as there are dangers in being insufficiently explicit. One cannot produce rules for doing fieldwork as if fieldwork were like a laboratory experiment. So complete and complex a human experience as fieldwork cannot be "programmed" in every detail. The personality, interests, strengths and weaknesses of each anthropologist differ. Similarly, an approach which might succeed admirably among gregarious Polynesians may fail altogether with the recalcitrant Nuer of the African Sudan. On the other hand, to provide no guidelines at all is to show too much confidence that young fieldworkers have a natural capacity to swim.

Anthropology has changed greatly since the early 1960's. Students today, like those of the past, still learn about fieldwork from informal discussions with each other and with their professors, and they still absorb a great deal from the courses they take on anthropological concepts and theories. But today, they also have access to a growing number of manuals on fieldwork as well as to personal accounts of the fieldwork experience, and they usually receive formal supervised training in fieldwork as part of their graduate and even undergraduate education. It may still be true, as so many anthropologists have said in the past, that the best predictor of success in fieldwork is the anthropologist's joy in anticipation of the task. But today anthropological training tends to weed out those who lack this interest and dedication before they ever leave the university to try their hand at independent fieldwork, and those who possess these attributes are no longer thrown into a sea of ethnographic confusion with nothing to keep them afloat except their determination.

Even in the early period, a few standard techniques such as the *genealogical method* of taking down *kin terms* were available to anthropologists who wished to use them in the field. One of the first attempts to help the fieldworker in a systematic way was the encyclopedic volume from the Royal Anthropological Institute of Great Britain and Ireland, entitled *Notes and Queries on Anthropology,* which was first published in 1874. This volume went into the field with most anthropologists. It was packed full of suggestions about what to look for and what questions to ask. Almost no detail was too minor. For example, consider this on *string* from the 1954 edition:

Inquire what substances are employed for the manufacture of the various kinds of string, and if they are subject to any preparation before or after manufacture. Are any animals or insects kept for the purpose of supplying materials to be spun? Are any plants cultivated for the sake of their fibre? If dyes are employed, how are they obtained and applied? Describe all methods of joining ends. Describe the methods of making worked strings. Is string made by women or men, or both? How long does each process take to produce a given length? (1954:286)

No matter how thorough a manual like this may be, new problems and interests soon demand new questions. *Notes and Queries on Anthropology* has been revised six times to date. Other manuals are now also available. One is Murdock's *Outline of Cultural Materials* (1950), which lists both general categories (such as diet, settlement pattern, and *ethnobotany)* for the fieldworker to investigate and also more specific categories. This manual, too, has been revised several times. There are also manuals devoted to the study of specialized subjects: kinship, language, and others. Probably the most extensively used of these is the *Field Guide for the Study of Socialization* (Whiting *et al.*, 1968).

Anthropology as a Science

In anthropological training an important consideration is the nature of anthropological inquiry itself and of the facts anthropologists hope to assemble in their fieldwork. Anthropologists generally recognize that our knowledge of the "real" world is difficult to obtain and is rarely certain. Einstein put it well when he said: "As far as the laws of mathematics refer to reality, they are not certain; and as far as they are certain, they do not refer to reality" (1953:189). This same point of view is reflected in the philosophical position that, strictly speaking, nothing can ever be proven true; it can only be proven false. In anthropology, as in other sciences, we often come to assume that a theory is true because we lack any competing theory that appears to be any better. But all scientists know that some day a better theory will come along and their "truest" theory will have to be modified or discarded altogether. To this extent, then, anthropologists recognize that knowledge of the world is uncertain and that this knowledge will undergo continuing revision as more becomes known about that world. But they hold to their assumption, which Einstein shared, that the world of reality can be understood, however imperfectly, and that the nature of this world can be agreed upon.

Agreement between observers concerning the world of reality—*intersubjectivity*—is by no means a simple accomplishment where complex human affairs are concerned, but neither is it impossible. Imagine yourself one of 100,000 spectators at a football game. Despite the emotion of a hot contest and the diverse backgrounds of the fans, certain events during the game are likely to be agreed upon by most, if not all: what time the game started, what color the uniforms were, whether rain was falling, whether a pass was complete to a receiver who caught it chest high standing all alone, whether a touchdown was scored by a man who fielded a kickoff and ran untouched right down the center of the field, and the like. But there might well be little agreement on whether a close pass-interference penalty was justified, whether a runner stepped out of bounds, whether a pass was caught fairly or trapped, whether the winning team in a close contest "really" deserved to win, and like matters. But what happens in a football game is relatively simple and clear-cut compared to most everyday human activities. The complexity of human life may be suggested by the movie *Rashomon* or by a play of Luigi Pirandello, in which each person involved sees an event in a somewhat different way. The anthropologist must decide how he can be sure that what he thinks took place in the field, *really* took place.

Anthropologists as recorders of objective reality, of facts, must attempt to eliminate the influence of *observer bias* in their fieldwork. Control over such bias is a central issue in fieldwork. Because what we see is so often related to our preconceptions or theories, our emotions (or what we want to see) may also influence our observations. A famous case in point involves the Pueblo Indians of the Southwest. Several anthropologists, but most notably Ruth Benedict, characterized these Indians as "Apollonian" in reference to their emotional restraint and their avoidance of violence or even of quarrels. Others wondered how she could have overlooked what were to them obvious examples of aggression, drunkenness, and emotional excess. For example, as to one item of Pueblo culture, Benedict (1934:83) said that the Hopi practice of whipping children during initiation ceremonies was really quite mild. "The lash does not draw blood . . . . The adults repudiate with distress the idea that the whips might raise welts." Other anthropologists found this whipping to be anything but mild; indeed, a Hopi Indian, Sun Chief, wrote in his autobiography that the lashing he received during his initiation had left him with permanent scars (Simmons, 1942:83):

I stood them fairly well, without crying, and thought my suffering was past; but then the Ho Katchina struck me four more times and cut me to pieces. I struggled, yelled, and urinated. . . . Blood was running down over my body.

After much debate involving the "facts" of each anthropologist's interpretation, it became clear that in addition to differences in rapport and fieldwork conditions, differences in bias were also involved. All of the anthropologists involved were attempting to be "objective" but the differences in their theoretical and emotional approach to Pueblo culture led to bias in what they observed and in how they interpreted what they observed. A second famous disagreement, in which Robert Redfield found the Mexican village of Tepoztlan to be almost idyllic while Oscar Lewis reported conflict, mayhem, and hostility, is another illustration of the same problem. Still another is the different interpretation of Ifugao religion by R. F. Barton and Father Lambrecht. Both men spent years with the Ifugao, a Philippine society, both were fluent in the language, and both described almost exactly the same things; yet the interpretation of the facts by Lambrecht, a priest, is considerably different from that of Barton, who was much more of an anthropologist.

One thing is indisputable. Francis Bacon, champion of the inductive method in science, was wrong in his belief that if a scientist were merely to collect all the facts, these facts would somehow speak for themselves. Social and cultural facts require some kind of interpretation before one can even know which ones to look for out of the infinite number possible. To make the interpretation requires a frame of reference or a point of view. As the philosopher Abraham Kaplan (1964:132-133) put it, "After the moment of the observer's birth no observation can be undertaken in all innocence. We always know something already, and this knowledge is intimately involved in what we come to know next, whether by observation or in any other way."

To a considerable extent, it is true that what you look for is what you see. In our own society we take notice of some things and events while missing others altogether. For example, in a restaurant we can easily tell a waitress from the patrons by her uniform, but when we want to order more bread and we look around for our particular waitress we often realize that we cannot recognize her. Her individual physical characteristics were not relevant before; now they are. What then do anthropologists look for?

Their general training in anthropology courses is very important. The anthropologist is taught to try out theories or hypotheses which compete with his own while he is in the field to be sure he is not overlooking or misinterpreting significant facts. He is cautioned in reporting facts to make clear what kinds of observations they are based on and the conditions under which they were made. Other safeguards include the use of more than one anthropologist in the fieldwork to complement and check one another. As fieldwork procedures become more and more explicit and precise, it becomes possible for anthropologists to replicate the work of others and to reach the same conclusions. Although there have been relatively few such restudies of the same culture, some have been carried out with sufficient agreement between the studies to suggest that bias can be controlled.

Camera, movie film, and tape recordings can also help the fieldworker to be objective, and students are taught how to use all these techniques for gathering data. The fact remains, however, that the anthropologist decides what the camera will watch or what the tape recorder will listen to. Technology is an aid to accurate observation, but it still takes a human brain to probe, discover, and explain the cultural pattern behind the human events that are recorded.

Planning for Fieldwork

In the early days of anthropology, anthropologists usually arrived in the field with little knowledge of the people they had come to study, uncertain what new cultural forms they might find. Margaret Mead, whose well-known book *Sex and Temperament in Three Primitive Societies* (1935) attempted to demonstrate that physiology does not dictate that sex roles will be the same in all societies, confessed that only purely by luck had she happened upon three societies so different in their sexual roles and therefore so perfect for her study. Anthropologists continue to be surprised when they arrive in the field, but many more societies have now been described and the anthropologist is far more likely to know what he may expect to find than was the case when Mead first went to New Guinea.

In the past, when most of the world's societies had never been studied at all, many anthropologists elected simply to describe everything that they could in the community they were studying. Quite a few, especially those who studied under Boas, were also working on a specific problem. A general question such as Margaret Mead's (whether or not sex roles were so physiologically determined that women in all societies would be maternal and submissive and men strong and warlike) can be tested only in certain types of societies that provide the necessary

A

B

C

D

ANTHROPOLOGISTS' DWELLINGS IN THE FIELD. (a) A temporary camp in southern Tanzania (R. B. Edgerton). (b) A house of local materials in the New Guinea Highlands (L. L. Langness). (c) The entrance to a cave occupied by an anthropologist, his wife, and daughter while working with the Tarahumara Indians of northern Mexico (courtesy of J. G. Kennedy). (d) House used for research with the Eskimo of western Alaska (courtesy of Wendell O. Oswalt).

data. The choice of a problem to study and a society to study it in go hand in hand. The most successful fieldwork usually occurs when the anthropologist takes care in choosing a significant problem (as we will discuss further in Part II of this book), then decides what data he can gather to prove or disprove the hypotheses he makes, and where he can best carry out his study.

It is usually advisable for the anthropologist to have a problem in mind before going into the field, where he or she will be virtually cut off from books and colleagues. At home, with a library available, one can read about theories, learn techniques, and study previous work on the problem. One can also consult with colleagues for helpful suggestions. It is unfortunately the case that many times an anthropologist, not being completely prepared to deal with a particular problem, returns from the field with gaps in his data that make it impossible to explain what he saw. Since time is always scanty in a field situation, the less time wasted trying to decide what kind of data to collect and devising techniques for collecting it, the more time is free for other necessary work.

Although Mead felt she needed to work in at least three societies for her study on sex and temperament, anthropologists have traditionally chosen to do a careful study in depth of just one society, dealing with all the significant aspects of the culture that relate to their problem. They usually do a general description of the society as well, so that they may have confidence that they understand what is actually going on and that they have not overlooked concealed or important facts. This is the essence of the principle of holism.

Selection of a specific society in which to work may sometimes be put off by the anthropologist until he arrives in the country of choice and decides between possible alternatives. Some of the factors he may consider include the following: whether the community is close to a major center (and hence so strongly influenced by it that the anthropologist will have to study both of the communities); whether the community may have been so strongly influenced by some historical event or catastrophe that all other causative factors which the anthropologist wishes to study are overshadowed by the impact of that event; whether the size and degree of modernization of the community suit the problem he is studying; whether the field location is feasible in terms of such practical considerations as availability of supplies and housing; and whether a stranger may expect a friendly reception by the society. In the early days of fieldwork, anthropologists were free to choose almost any spot on the globe which caught their interest or needed to be described. Since that time, political conflict has often closed large areas of the world to anthropology. Until 1972, all the People's Republic of China was off-limits to Americans; the Soviet Union still is, as are several countries in the so-called Third World.

Most anthropologists know a great deal about the community or area they are going to live in long before they ever set foot on the scene. They read other anthropologist's accounts of the society if such exist; they pore over traveler's journals, missionary records and local newspapers to compile some picture of the society, both past and present. Background reading is an acknowledged help to the anthropologist, but he should examine the work of others critically. There is always the danger that an unwary anthropologist may build up a set of expectations about an area that will prevent him from seeing its culture with a fresh point of view. For example, on the basis of his reading, the fieldworker may begin doing his research with the assumption that the society has a clear-cut *matrilineal* clan system when in fact the situation is actually a good deal more complex and subtle. Hopefully a good fieldworker will discover the truth before it is too late. Thus, Marvin Harris (1968:585-586) reports that when he did fieldwork among the Bathonga of Mozambique, he was convinced by his reading of the eminent anthropologist Radcliffe-Brown that these people had a particular kind of kinship system. Because of this preconception, it took Harris a long time to discover that the facts of the Bathonga system were a good deal more complex and ambiguous than the "authority," Radcliffe-Brown, had made them out to be. Every an-thropologist is expected to read extensively before fieldwork, but with an aware-ness that misleading preconceptions are easy to form.

The languages spoken in the small nonliterate societies to which anthropologists typically go are seldom taught or even known in the West. If an anthropologist has the opportunity to learn the native language before he goes to the field, he usually seizes upon it. Language is obviously an important means of communication in fieldwork, but, more than that, it provides a window into the emotional and intellectual world of the people and their culture. Most anthropologists cannot learn the native language beforehand, so they have to settle for learning a trade language or "pidgin," if one is used in the area where they will be working, or they must allow time for learning the language after reaching the field, or they must rely on English-speaking interpreters. Often they do all of these.

Only a few anthropologists are gifted enough in learning languages to become more than minimally competent in the native language, since most field trips are limited by finances and by academic schedules to about a year. A manual (Gudschinsky, 1967) has been prepared in an effort to help anthropologists learn languages more rapidly and efficiently. Some anthropologists believe that the only means of acquiring adequate linguistic proficiency is to put immediate and total reliance on the native language. When one must learn to speak the native language in order to deal with all one's needs, one learns, they say, to speak as a child does—rapidly and well. But not all anthropologists are willing to learn a language in this way, and not all people may be willing to tolerate bumbling efforts. For example, Laura Bohannan reports that her efforts to learn the language during her early days of fieldwork among the Tiv were almost disastrous. The Tiv organized their language lessons for her by assembling various leaves for her to name. Reluctantly, she began to name them (1964:15-16):

I spoke more loudly; my pronunciation couldn't be that bad. Ikpoom's eyes grew sadder; the women seemed incredulous. The little boy could bear it no longer. He snatched from me the leaf I was naming and handed me another. The order had been mixed, and not once had I put the right name to the right plant.

These people are farmers: to them plants are as important and familiar as people. I'd never been on a farm and am not even sure which are begonias, dahlias or petunias. Plants, like algebra, have a habit of looking alike and being different, or looking different and being alike; consequently mathematics and botany confused me. For the first time in my life I found myself in a community where ten-year-old children weren't my mathematical superiors. I also found myself in a place where every plant, wild or cultivated, had a name and a use, and where every man, woman and child knew literally hundreds of plants. None of them could ever believe that I could not if I only would.

Fortunately, Bohannan eventually overcame this bad start.   There is no easy solution to the problem of language learning. Some fieldwork problems demand a solid working knowledge of the native language; others do not. Some anthropologists have written superb accounts of their fieldwork despite their almost total ignorance of the language. Others who have known the language very well have produced nothing of merit. All can agree that knowledge of the native language is an important tool for any fieldworker. Wherever possible he should acquire it, but good fieldwork will also continue to be done by anthropologists who for one reason or another do not learn the language of the people they study. To a certain extent the necessity for language proficiency depends upon the problem to be researched. If, for example, one is embarked on a study of economic change which involves such things as counting the numbers of livestock or measuring the size of fields, fluency in the local language is not so critical as it will be if one is studying beliefs about supernatural beings or collecting information on marriage and divorce.

The anthropologist must also keep alive in his chosen field location. In some fieldwork no amount of planning and care can produce comfort; survival is all one can hope for. Anthropologists who study pastoral nomads in the Middle East or hunters and gatherers in tropical forests or the Arctic often must endure great physical and psychological privation. The dedication of these anthropologists is dramatically documented by their work. For example, read Philip Gulliver's account of his attempts merely to keep up with the pastoral Turkana of Kenya's remote, hot, and arid northern frontier (1966), or Allan Holmberg's ordeal by hunger among the hunting and gathering Sirionó of Bolivia (1969), who themselves lived perpetually on the edge of starvation, or Jean Briggs's account of cold and psychological privation among the Eskimo of the Canadian Arctic (1970). Perhaps the too literally chilling words of an Eskimo woman to Jean Briggs say as much as is necessary on this subject (1970:19): "It's very cold down there—*very cold*. If I were going to be at Back River this winter, I would like to adopt you and try to keep you alive."

But not all anthropologists do fieldwork under such difficult physical conditions. Some, in fact, choose villages in Spain or Greece, or lovely Pacific Islands, and the majority work in places where reasonable planning and precaution can cope with weather and even with insects, scorpions, snakes, and a host of unfamiliar diseases. To be sure, anthropologists collect tropical illnesses much as other professionals develop ulcers; a few have died during fieldwork (usually by reason of accident, poor judgment, or carelessness, only rarely as a result of hostility). The experienced anthropologist takes into account his personal needs—for privacy, companionship, warmth, cleanliness, and the like—then chooses a field situation in which he can best function.

Physical hardships are real enough but the greatest hazards are psychological. There is some discussion of several psychological hazards in the next section.

Where fieldwork is concerned, practical considerations can be just as important as intellectual ones. Some anthropologists are so casual about their arrangements that friends would think they were leaving for a weekend camping trip, not a year in Borneo. Others agree with an experienced British anthropologist that "any damn fool can be uncomfortable in the bush," and lay their plans with meticulous care. Whatever the individual style of the anthropologist, some practical considerations are essential. There must be money for the field trip. It may come from a research foundation, a university grant, or private savings—all three sources are common—but money must be available to cover the costs of travel, equipment, supplies, and salaries for workers in the field. Money often limits the time the anthropologist can spend in the field.

Anthropologists with families are faced with the question of whether or not to bring them along. The rigors of the field are frequently severe and an anthropologist working alone may be both freer to move about and less of a burden on the community. But there is often a strong advantage to having a family in the field. The presence of children soon convinces people that the anthropologist intends no harm, and having a wife or husband will define the anthropologist's sex status in the community. Furthermore, in the small societies which an anthropologist typically visits, the social world of men and women is often clearly divided and half the community, to varying degrees, may be inaccessible unless both a man and a woman do the fieldwork. There is also the comfort that a family can provide when the anthropologist feels far removed from the comforts of his own culture and those who understand how he really thinks and feels.

The process of getting immunizations, visas, technical equipment and medical supplies can be time-consuming, but such arrangements are necessary as are the details of setting up working relationships within a foreign country. Careful attention to getting governmental permissions and clearances as well as introductions to local politicians, religious leaders, and cooperating scholars may save an anthropologist weeks and even months of cooling his heels in government offices when he is eager to be out and at work in a community.

The wise anthropologist makes contingency plans as well as checking and double checking his basic plans. Because they go where few others have, anthropologists often do not find what was expected—one graduate student recently arrived at her destination only to discover that the whole community had been transplanted to another country by a large manufacturing concern. Few surprises are as great as this, but many anthropologists have had to change their plans considerably and show great flexibility once in the field. It is in just such situations, with libraries far away, that the anthropologist most rely upon the concepts and methods he has been taught. Improvisation cannot succeed without a foundation in training.

Entering the Field

Fieldwork begins with first contact. Here anthropologist Napoleon Chagnon tells us about his first meeting with the warlike Yąnomamö Indians who live in the tropical forest region of South America:

It was hot and muggy, and my clothing was soaked with perspiration. It clung uncomfortably to my body, as it did thereafter for the remainder of the work. The small,biting gnats were out in astronomical numbers, for it was the beginning of the dry season. My face and hands were swollen from the venom of their numerous stings. In just a few moments I was to meet my first Yąnomamö, my first primitive man. What would it be like? I had visions of entering the village and seeing 125 social facts running about calling each other kinship terms and sharing food, each waiting and anxious to have me collect his genealogy . . . . The excitement of meeting my first Indians was almost unbearable as I duck-waddled through the low passage into the village clearing.

I looked up and gasped when I saw a dozen burly, naked, filthy, hideous men staring at us down the shafts of their drawn arrows! Immense wads of green tobacco were stuck between their lower teeth and lips, making them look even more hideous, and strands of dark-green slime dripped or hung from their noses. We arrived at the village while the men were blowing a hallucinogenic drug up their noses. One of the side affects of the drug is a runny nose. The mucus is always saturated with the green powder and the Indians usually let it run freely from their nostrils. My next discovery was that there were a dozen or so vicious, underfed dogs snapping at my legs, circling me as if I were going to be their next meal. I just stood there holding my notebook, helpless and pathetic. Then the stench of the decaying vegetation and filth struck me and I almost got sick. I was horrified. What sort of welcome was this for the person who came here to live with you and learn your way of life, to become friends with you? (Chagnon, 1968:4-5)

Chagnon's reception among the Yąnomamö may not have been precisely what what he had hoped for, but after the initial shock wore off, he settled in for nineteen months of difficult and physically demanding fieldwork, then returned to write detailed accounts. Sometimes, if not often, a society altogether rejects outsiders who try to enter. Evans-Pritchard, the noted British anthropologist, met with a hostile reception from the Nuer and never did entirely succeed in overcoming their suspicions of him. The Pueblo Indians, during an especially trying period in their history, cast out anthropologists who came to study them for the slightest infractions of cultural rules or else rejected them totally at the outset. Perhaps the real surprise is that so many societies do accept a strange-looking intruder, perhaps with a family, and take him or her in to live with them.

Being taken into a community means that the anthropologist is usually involved in the give and take of community life, including helping out in any way he can. He exchanges gifts and food; he uses his limited medical knowledge; he gives affection and companionship and often tries to influence the government on behalf of "his" people. This highly personal mode of reciprocity is especially frequent in small nonliterate societies. Peggy Golde's experience in a Mexican village is a good example:

What was borne in on me repeatedly was that *all* transactions in this village ultimately had to be reciprocal. Every offer or act of help carried the expectation of some return, either immediate or at some time in the future. Since I could not reciprocate by helping with the harvest, with food preparation for fiestas, with rounding up animals, or with homebuilding—the traditional exchanges—I repaid with money or with food, gifts of cloth, knives, books, and most importantly, medical care. I paid dues to the pueblo like any villager, gave candles and incense to the church, bought a dictionary for the secretary of the pueblo, loaned stationery and stamps, changed money and even loaned it to good friends, and interceded with government officials on behalf of the people; in these ways I demonstrated not only my usefulness, worth, and importance, but also the fact that I could be counted on to keep up my end of the "bargain." (1970:83)

Some anthropologists, especially ones who work with more westernized societies, refuse to begin fieldwork unless they are certain that they are giving as much to the people as they believe the people are giving to them. Such arrangements often are informally, or even formally, contractual, the people and the anthropologist reaching explicit agreement on what he will do and how this will benefit the people. For example, an urban cooperative may invite an anthropologist to work with them in developing better ways of working together, or a tribe of South American Indians may invite an anthropologist to live with them in order better to protect them against economic encroachment or political exploitation. Sometimes, it appears, an anthropologist can be wanted although no one is sure just quite why, as in K. E. Read's pioneering fieldwork in the Eastern Highlands of New Guinea:

When Young-Whitforde asked him his business Makis quickly assured him that none of his people were in trouble. He had come alone and on his own initiative, he said, to ask the government for a white man. At first Young-Whitforde thought he referred to one of the several Europeans who were looking for land in the valley; but Makis answered that this was not the kind of man he wanted. Further questioning was unable to elicit a more definite statement of his wishes. He became embarrassed and said that the government ought to know the kind of man to give him. . . .

There were times in the next two years when I credited him with nothing but cupidity, knowing, even when I thought it, that this was unjust to him, that there was much more in his wanting me than the very moderate material benefits I was able to provide. The noticeable difference between myself and other Europeans lent his group and himself, as my mentor, a useful prestige, and it soon became apparent that I had to be wary of attempts to enlist the influence I was presumed, quite wrongly, to have at the District Office. It was necessary to refuse the flattering requests to write letters explaining the merits of a pending court case because, as he put it, I knew the local customs. Yet this, too, was only incidental to something else he hoped to gain. . . . I began to feel that his request had been his commitment to the future, a reaching out for one among many possible untried guidelines to tomorrow . . . . (1965:14-15).

One of the first things that the natives want to know is what the anthropologist really is and why he wants to live with them. Even before entering a society, most anthropologists have chosen a role. They usually try to find a role and an explanation for their presence in which they will be seen as a harmless but curious stranger who has come to learn the native ways. Few people in the preliterate world can be expected to understand the role of the scholar in search of knowledge; it is common for these people to suspect the anthropologist of being a tax collector, missionary, or whatever other role "white men" commonly play. The anthropologist's public role will undergo continual revision as he makes friends and enemies throughout his fieldwork, but if he sticks to his role, is kind, harmless, and helpful, he will probably be able to overcome suspicion and opposition sufficiently to allow his work to proceed. Very few anthropologists, if any, have practiced the kinds of deception used by John Howard Griffin, who dyed himself brown to see how it felt to be a Negro (1960); or by Morris West, who dressed in rags to observe children in the streets of Naples (1957); or by several sociologists who in order to study enlisted men in the Air Force used an Air Force officer as a fieldworker, giving him a new name, birthdate, personal history and mannerisms, not to mention minor surgery and a diet so that he would appear to be 18 years old instead of 26 (Sullivan, Queen, and Patrick, 1958). Anthropologists are often misunderstood, and they may engage in minor deceptions simply because of the confusion of their role as scholars, but major deceptions of this kind would be neither ethical nor practical.

As the anthropologist and his family are incorporated into the social fabric of a community, they may be adopted by the people they live with, since most of the work of small societies is organized along the lines of kinship, with all the rights, duties, and obligations contingent upon such relations. An anthropologist usually tries to proceed with caution in these matters, for he may find himself being drawn into the quarrels, bickering, and factionalism that often occur in small communities. If he does, then his ability to collect unbiased information may diminish, because as he becomes closer to some people in the community, he moves farther away from others, making it more difficult to collect information equally from all. Alan Beals compared two fieldwork situations in India in which he was involved—one in which he stood apart somewhat as an impartial observer, and the other in which he was pulled completely into the social life of the community. Of the latter he comments, ''They were unaccustomed to strangers and they would not let us remain strangers'' (1970:45). Beals speculates that a person who tried to stand apart in such a situation might bring on the very reaction he was trying to avoid, simply because his behavior would be out of the ordinary and would make people uneasy.

One of the earliest and most common experiences of the anthropologist who attempts to immerse himself in another society is a feeling of cultural disorientation. He wants to be socially accepted by the people he has come to study, but they may not respond to his overtures in predictable ways. He in turn is uncertain how he should translate their cultural signals and respond to them. Among the Bedouin of Saudi Arabia, the anthropologist may be invited into the sheik's tent to explain his mission. The sheik courteously plies the anthropologist with cup after cup of a heavy sweet coffee, politely exchanging news of the area. The anthropologist begins to feel acute social discomfort. How many cups of coffee must he drink to avoid offending the hospitality of the sheik? How can he indicate that the honored guest can drink no more? How do they get to the point of their talk? Should the guest signal when he is ready to leave, or would that be rude? He knows that a great deal hinges on his interview with the sheik but he doesn't know how to guide its outcome. The smallest actions become significant to the newly arrived anthropologist and a source of apprehension and potential embarrassment. He watches people and tries to imitate them; the people in turn soon realize, often with great amazement, that here is an adult who has not learned even the most elementary things that every child knows. Of his first day in the Indian village of Gopalpur, Beals recalls:

> In a surprisingly short time, we were painfully aware that we had achieved an almost legendary reputation for incompetence. We could not get water, we could not make fire. We seemed totally unable to get food or prepare it properly once we had it. (1970:38)

The uneasiness brought about by living in an unpredictable social world, combined with the loss of one's own comfortable social world, brings on a condition known as *culture shock*—the shock of passing from a familiar to an unknown culture. It is therefore not to be wondered at that in the face of culture shock the fieldworker often retreats for a period from any social interactions. Instead, he may spend recuperative periods in the company of his family, or with the box of novels that every anthropologist is cautioned to bring, or else flee into the nearest town for a while to cushion the psychological impact of a social world gone awry.

The fieldworker may be determined to try to live within the value system of the people so that he may come to understand it with an insider's knowledge. The intention may put him to a degree of effort; some cultures will be fairly congenial to his personality while others will try him sorely. For example, in some areas of the world it is almost literally impossible to bathe, defecate, or make love in private. Some anthropologists may be able to tolerate the lack of privacy well, but most find it hard to adjust. These problems are vividly illustrated by the experiences of Robert and Ruth Dentan among the Semai of Malaya (Dentan, 1970:104-105):

> The notion of privacy is rather alien to the Semai, except insofar as people of opposite sexes are not supposed to spy in order to see each other's naked genitals. For us to tell a man with whom we had a good relationship that we did not want to see him at a certain time, simply because we wanted to be alone, would have been a gross, incomprehensible insult. He would have been put in a state of ritual danger, and, if he did not feel that we had terminated our relationship with him, he would almost certainly have broken it off himself. On the other hand, as bourgeois Americans, we were used to houses with thick-walled rooms that insulate an individual or couple from others, so that the inhabitants can be alone to think, read, write, or perform "intimate" biological activities. We found it inhibiting, for example, when trying to indulge in a little connubial bliss in our creaky house, when Uproar, our next door neighbor, would shout jokingly, "Hey, what are you two doing in there?"

The Dentans eventually managed to live without their accustomed privacy. However, they go on to report,

> . . . we were working from 5 or 6 a.m. to 11 or 12 p.m. every day at jobs that were often intellectually, emotionally, and/or physically exhausting. We needed an occasional break just to keep going. After about a month, we hit on the idea of a weekly "taboo day," on which we were "ritually unable" to do much socializing unless something unusual happened or visitors came from another settlement. The Semai, knowing of the Malay sabbath, could understand this sort of ritual restriction. Although we were never able to have a completely uninterrupted "taboo day," we were able to get in a little reading, sleeping, and letter-writing.

These may appear to be commonsense considerations, but they are important and should not be made light of. Successful fieldwork depends upon the trained sensitivity of the anthropologist. If the anthropologist is sick, depressed, or lonely, his sensitivity to the people around him will be blunted or distorted and his ability to observe and record a people's way of life will be reduced.

It is important that the anthropologist record first impressions. Life in any strange society is at first a kaleidoscope of new, unusual, even mysterious activities. First impressions can provide valuable information that will go quite unnoticed once this new world becomes more familiar. The commonsense everyday understandings that enable social life to continue will soon be as much taken for granted by the anthropologist as they are by the people themselves. People who experience the bewildering impact of a new cultural world tend to try to understand it by waiting, sorting out impressions, and finally becoming accustomed to it. This is what most of us do when we are tourists. For the anthropologist, waiting is a mistake.

Many anthropologists keep a diary. Probably they all should. If the anthropologist keeps a daily diary in which he records his thoughts, impressions, and the circumstances under which he collected his data, he is then in a position to discover, for example, that when ''Juan'' told him a peculiar fact which does not fit with the rest of what he knows, Juan was in the midst of a quarrel with ''Carlos,'' the man in whose house the anthropologist was staying. In this and similar ways, the diary becomes a valuable resource for evaluating data, sources, and the anthropologist's own state of being when he was making observations—an important variable in the quality of his descriptions.

As we see so easily in the diary of Malinowski (1967), his frequent illnesses and bouts of melancholia could have affected the way in which he conducted his fieldwork among the Trobriand Islanders. Consider the following entry for November 26, 1917 (Malinowski, 1967:131):

Yesterday I had what is usually called *an attack of feverishness, a touch of fever*. Physical and mental sluggishness. Yesterday, for instance, I felt no desire and was not strong enough to take a walk, not even around the Island. Nor have I the energy to get to work, not even to write letters to E.R.M. or look over my ethnographic notes. Moreover, I am extremely *irritable* and the yells of the boys and other noises get horribly on my nerves. The moral tonus is also considerably lower. Emotional bluntness—I think of E.R.M. less intensely than usual. Resistance to lecherous thoughts weaker. Clarity of metaphysical conception of the world completely dimmed: I cannot endure being with myself, my thoughts pull me down to the surface of the world. I am unable to control things or to be creative in relation to the world. Tendency to read *rubbish*; I leaf through a magazine. I seek out the company of various people.

Malinowski was unique as a fieldworker only by having his diary published (posthumously, we might add). All anthropologists have their bad days. A diary helps them to understand how the way they felt that day may have been related to what they observed. The fieldworker's diary should also contain an account of what was done during the day, and a record of new ideas, puzzles, and problems as they come up. It can also be helpful to jot down one's plans for the following day. Keeping a diary is hard work; and when conditions are difficult and one is tired, only the most disciplined fieldworker can do so on a daily basis. Most agree, however, that a well-kept diary is of immense value, not only while one is in the field, but also in making sense of one's data after leaving the field.

The way that the anthropologist views the busy social scene in his community might be likened to the way a drama critic thinks of a play. Individuals take or are given roles according to their characteristics. They learn these roles—but interpret them according to their own personalities—and perform them in scenes, events, and acts that are linked together in meaningful time sequences. A general cultural plot as well as a series of individual subplots run through the action. But there is a critical difference between stage drama and real life—in real life the actors and outside events can affect the direction the script takes. Nothing is predetermined.

The anthropologist has the problem of discovering how much of the drama unfolding before him follows cultural guidelines. He must find out how much can be attributed to individual idiosyncrasy, how much violates agreed-upon ways of playing a role, how much is fresh innovation, and he must learn how many alternatives there are for playing a role, responding in a scene, and rearranging events. Who can be chosen to play a role and what characteristics must he or she have? How will his or her role interpretation be judged by others? Above all, what is the set of stage directions that exists for the actors, where did the directions come from, and how widely are they shared?

Many anthropologists agree that learning the stage coordinates of the scenes enacted—the significant props and the places where people are typically located in the space—can be done early and will be most useful throughout fieldwork. Also collecting a complete list of the players, their characteristics, and some of their basic roles aids the anthropologist in making sense of events and scenes. In many small nonliterate societies, roles are assigned and activities are organized primarily in accordance with kinship statuses. Therefore, in addition to mapping, and taking a simple preliminary census, most anthropologists will attempt to take a set of genealogies that will display basic kinship relations and set down the expected rights and duties attached to each kinship status. All these activities—mapping, census-taking, and genealogical inquiry—can usually be conducted soon after arrival, even with limited language facility, and they lay an invaluable foundation for the rest of the anthropologist's fieldwork.

Census-Taking and Mapping

A census can often be conducted early in the field research, especially if the census items are few and innocuous, pertaining, for example, only to the name, age, sex, and kinship affiliation of each member of the household. Such data can sometimes be collected by the fieldworker himself when he is introduced to members of the community. It can also be collected by local field assistants and can thereby serve as an early means of checking on these assistants' accuracy and reliability. In either event, the census data should be rechecked periodically to take account of changes in household composition as individual households progress through their cycles of establishing families and breaking up, and also to take account of shifts in population which signal changes in birthrates, death rates, and migration rates.

Some field censuses are elaborate, containing questions about marriage payments, stillbirths, miscarriages, economic transactions, economic holdings, religious beliefs, and the like. This sort of census almost certainly *cannot* be conducted early in the fieldwork without arousing suspicion or hostility.

In some field situations, even the most innocent census inquiries may create suspicion and resistance. In certain communities any enumeration of the population may conjure up visions of government taxation. In others, names of the dead cannot safely or decently be spoken. In many communities, questions about economic practices or possessions are likely to be resisted. And in some communities, people simply refuse to cooperate at all with an inquisitive foreigner. Evans-Pritchard's classic encounter with the haughty and suspicious Nuer cattleherders of the Sudan is an illustration of how bad matters can sometimes become (1940:12-13:

I (Evans-Pritchard): Who are you?
Cuol: A man.
I: What is your name?
Cuol: Do you want to know my *name*?
I: Yes.
Cuol: You want to know *my* name?
I: Yes, you have come to visit me in my tent and I would like to know who you are.
Cuol: All right. I am Cuol. What is your name?
I: My name is Pritchard.
Cuol: What is your father's name?
I: My father's name is also Pritchard.
Cuol: No, that cannot be true. You cannot have the same name as your father.
I: It is the name of my lineage. What is the name of your lineage?
Cuol: Do you want to know the name of my lineage?
I: Yes.
Cuol: What will you do with it if I tell you? Will you take it to your country?
I: I don't want to do anything with it. I just want to know it since I am living at your camp.
Cuol: Oh well, we are Lou.
I: I did not ask the name of your tribe. I know that. I am asking you the name of your lineage.
Cuol: Why do you want to know the name of my lineage?
I: I don't want to know it.
Cuol: Then why do you ask me for it? Give me some tobacco.

I defy the most patient ethnologist to make headway against this kind of opposition. One is just driven crazy by it. Indeed, after a few weeks of associating solely with Nuer one displays, if the pun be allowed, the most evident symptoms of "Nuerosis."

Fortunately, most communities are a good deal more cooperative than this one and the anthropologist can usually complete a map and brief census early in his fieldwork. Additional information is added throughout the fieldwork; and as the fieldworker's rapport and his knowledge grow, more sensitive and complicated information can be added.

In addition to identifying the native actors and their significant relationships, the anthropologist should attempt to locate people in space. Mapping such things as where persons live, which way their doors face, where their fields lie, the locations of the religious center, of water, of pasture, and so on, may help tell a story about the condition of present social relations in the community and may indicate some reasons for their coming about. Mapping physical features of the adjoining countryside may reveal problems which certain cultural practices have been designed to solve. And mapping neighboring groups and resources may point out important factors outside the community which nevertheless affect relationships within it.

In a settled village it is relatively simple to make a map, but if the anthropologist has taken up residence with a mobile tribe, each new camp site poses a potentially significant rearrangement of households and these rearrangements may carry social information about changed relationships. Old alliances break up, new ones are formed, and the spatial shape of camp life changes accordingly. Aerial maps and accompanying photographs can be a particularly rich source of information about life in such a community, and are valuable in any kind of field research.

Genealogical Method

In our own American society, mother, father, brother, sister, son, daughter, husband, and wife constitute some of our deepest and most meaningful relationships. However, in many important areas of life—school, job, and recreation —teachers, girl friends, boy friends, bosses, coworkers, and friends who are related neither by blood nor marriage may dominate our social scene. In small nonliterate societies this is seldom the case and kinship often does most of the work of organizing social, domestic, and economic relations.

The pattern of kin relations can seem strange and confusing to an anthropologist who has newly arrived in such a society. Consider, for instance, what Malinowski found when he did his celebrated fieldwork among the Trobriand Islanders of Melanesia. For a young boy in the Trobriands, "father" is the "man who is married to the boy's mother, who lives in the same house with her and forms part of the household" (1929:5). The "father" is not considered to be related to the youth, however, and he does not have the social and legal duties that "fathers" typically have in American society. These duties are instead taken by the mother's brother, the boy's uncle. The youth grows up in the village of his father and mother, but unless his mother's brother also lives in that village, the youth is considered an "outsider." "His" village, where he will eventually go to reside and where he will inherit land, is the village of his mother's brother. He may even be betrothed to one of his mother's brother's daughters. From this uncle the boy inherits his property, and to his sister makes a large gift of the produce he raises. The boy's father is a warm and loving figure who in his lifetime may attempt to freely give things to his son, yet his worldly goods are rightfully the property of his sister's sons, and it is these cousins of the boy who will eventually inherit from the father.

For an anthropologist brought up in American society, the complexities of kinship in such a situation can be confusing. Fortunately there is a technique which can come to his aid—the *genealogical method* of taking down a person's relatives. This technique was developed quite early in the history of anthropology by W. H. R. Rivers during the Torres Straits Expedition of 1901. Rivers's method is so clear and so thorough that it has continued almost unchanged from that time to the present as an integral part of most fieldwork.

Although not all communities will readily accept genealogical inquiry, most find it a topic of natural interest and a few find it highly enjoyable, so most anthropologists are able to carry out genealogical interviews early in their fieldwork. Using the genealogical method means asking each member of the society to name and state his relationship to all his kin. For example, the first question might be: "What is the name of the woman who gave birth to you?" which should produce the name of the informant's (known for this purpose as *ego*) biological mother. Once the anthropologist has ego's pedigree, he asks him what term he uses for each relative and they for him, and how he addresses them in person, and they him. Rivers also recommended that the informant be asked to list all persons to whom a given kinship term would apply. To complete a genealogical interview, the fieldworker would also investigate the various ways a kinship term may be used, whether it would change in certain social situations, and how people in various kinship relationships are expected to behave toward one another.

With this genealogical information, the anthropologist is able to see clearly which persons are ego's blood kin (*consanguineal* kin), and which are his kin by marriage (*affinal* kin). Putting all the pedigrees he collects together, he can make a chart showing all the kin connections between various members in the society, and with the information from his auxiliary questions about kinship roles, he can deduce how each person ought to act toward every other person in terms of kinship expectations.

A simple and concise manual describing the genealogical method as well as the uses for kinship information has recently been published by Schusky (1965).

Learning the Language

The set of kin terms which the anthropologist elicits by the genealogical method are labels with which the members of that culture classify and mark off categories of kin in a way which is significant for them. Knowing the kin terms helps the anthropologist see the world "through the eyes of the native." For example, anthropologists have discovered that when kin in two different biological relationships to an ego (for instance, the mother's father and the father's father) are nevertheless called by the same term ("grandfather" in our society), this terminology is usually an indication that they will be perceived by ego as sharing significant characteristics, either in terms of their social or economic roles or in their behavior towards ego.

In similar fashion, by learning the people's language the anthropologist learns the rest of the labels which they use to classify their world, and by learning them he comes closer to seeing the world as they do. The language sorts and labels social statuses (*shaman*, *sorcerer*, hunter, *talking chief*, and the like), telling us also what emotional connotations each has. The language draws attention to behaviors that bring forth the same response as being somehow similar in the eyes of the natives (a baby who spills its food is scolded with "shame!" and a child who teases another is also told "shame!"; both are considered to be cases of misbehavior). The language labels and classifies events (breakfast, lunch, and dinner are all "meals" in our society, but while each is a meal, each is also considered different and has a different label). Language focuses attention on important areas of culture, as when the proliferation of terms within a more general category allows people to be very specific about significant matters (the Eskimo have a multitude of terms to describe different kinds of snow). Language directs attention to important concepts guiding people's lives by the very frequency with which the same term reappears in conversations (the recurrent use of "honor" in many Mediterranean societies is one example). In short, knowledge of the language helps the anthropologist to unlock people's perceptual, emotional, and cognitive worlds.

Most anthropologists get to work on their language learning as soon as possible. Often this is not only a practical necessity but is also an excellent way to make use of one's time in the early days of fieldwork when it is frequently difficult to do anything else. The fieldworker can profitably spend time in language learning with a single person—sometimes even a child—while waiting for everyone to become more accustomed to him. And language learning is by no means as puzzling or threatening to most non-Western people as are many other kinds of inquiry (such as, for example, asking who is married to whom, what kind of sexual behavior is preferred, or how much land each person owns).

Finding Cultural Patterns

Anthropologists have many reasons for wishing to discover and understand the cultural patterns of the societies they study. Some want to describe the patterns before they pass out of existence. Some want to examine a particular theory. Others are interested in how cultural patterns change, how they relate to each other in a functioning system, or how people learn these patterns. Whatever the particular interest, each fieldworker must find a way to understand the many patterns that make up the new cultural world he has come to study.

One of the first ways that the anthropologist learns the cultural code is by being inducted into the culture himself as a participant-observer. In the early days of settling in, which we have described, the anthropologist may find himself in the privileged position of being excused for many of his social gaffes, although more often he finds himself in the rather unsettling position of being treated as a not-too-bright child in need of training. The training process gives him some of the fundamentals of the culture—some of the basic rules, forms of etiquette, important values, as well as some explanations of why things are done or what happens if they are not done. He is also constantly discovering new rules and expectations by clumsily or unintentionally breaking them. To one who observes well and asks the right questions, these early learning situations can reveal a great deal, since people will go out of their way to teach the anthropologist how to be socially appropriate and helpful rather than be a continuing embarrassment or burden. And though it is highly unlikely that the fieldworker will ever cease to be an outsider in the community he studies, this role can have advantages since, as Florence Kluckhohn (1941) noted, much valuable information may become available precisely because one is "outside" the culture.

As the fieldworker observes and participates, he becomes aware of the complexities and contradictions in what people say and in what they do. What people say is right and proper is referred to as *ideal culture*, and these ideals, or values as they are sometimes called, are an important insight into how and why people behave as they do. Yet the fieldworker will also discover that many people do not behave as their ideals would have them do. This behavior is also important not only because it points to the realities rather than ideals of life, but because it can give insights into areas of change or tension in the culture. Participant-observation permits the fieldworker to balance the real and the ideal in a way that other methods can seldom match.

For example, if one carries out an interview how can one be certain that people will behave as they say they would? This problem led the sociologist Richard LaPiere (1934) to conduct an instructive piece of research. LaPiere had been trained by Malinowski in the complexities of real versus ideal culture but he wanted to demonstrate for sociologists how discrepant the two could be. In the company of a Chinese married couple, who were his friends, he spent two years traveling around the United States staying at hotels and eating in restaurants. Despite the feelings about Chinese in the United States in the early 1930's when the research was done, they were refused service only once. Later, LaPiere wrote to the same establishments to ask if they would accept members of the "Chinese race" as guests. Only one answer was affirmative and that was from a woman who reminisced about the nice Chinese couple that had stayed there six months earlier. LaPiere showed that what people did could not necessarily be predicted from what they said. Participant-observation often permits the fieldworker to understand real and ideal culture in the same way that members of the culture do, thus avoiding the kind of confusion that LaPiere was illustrating. The method also gives insight into how well cultural ideals are followed, how they are enforced, what happens to people who violate them, and how various situations cause rules and behavior to be modified.

Participant-observation also offers safeguards against one of the major problems of anthropology, *reactivity*. Reactivity refers to the effect that an observer (or any kind of investigator) has upon the phenomenon he is attempting to study. LaPiere's research with the Chinese couple, for example, apparently influenced the verbal behavior of the one lady who answered affirmatively. Reactivity has been reported for inanimate as well as animate phenomena, as, for example, in the well-known *Heisenberg undertainty principle* (Webb *et al.*, 1966). All sciences have this problem, but none more so than the social sciences whose objects of study are fellow human beings. Human beings have an impressive ability to guess what social scientists want from them and to alter their behavior to please, confuse, or deceive those who have the audacity to "study" them. Many of the methods of modern social science are designed to cope with this "reaction" on the part of its "objects" of study. But no technique has proven so effective in this regard as prolonged participant-observation. The annals of anthropology are filled with accounts or people who were still attempting to deceive an anthropologist after a year of more of fieldwork, but as time goes on such efforts are less and less successful. Living with a people makes it impossible for them to hide everything, and the longer one lives with them, the more difficult their efforts to deceive become. Since these deceptive people themselves are aware of the difficulties in maintaining their deception in the face of an anthropologist who has come to stay—seemingly forever—people often abandon deception or pretense and behave as naturally as they ever would. It is probably correct to say that all people sometimes hide certain things from everyone they can, sometimes even from themselves; but the longer one lives with people and the better one knows them, the less likely it is that the presence of the investigator will produce unknown effects upon the behavior the investigator is attempting to understand. Being aware of reactivity and deception can, however, lead to amusing, awkward, and even dangerous situations. As the anthropologist comes to know what things the people wish to keep from others such as government officials or missionaries, he or she may at times be present when they deliberately falsify something to someone else. Thus the anthropologist is faced with the choice of either giving away the false-hood or remaining silent. If his knowledge involves something important like, say, hiding a critically ill person, protecting a murderer, or planning a murder, the fieldworker needs to make an extremely difficult decision.

Beyond Participant-Observation

Participant-observation endures as a fundamental approach in anthropology because it permits the fieldworker to see life as it is being lived, and to understand it by actually living it as much as possible. And participant-observation does so with the smallest amount of disruption to the lives of the people being studied. Thus it comes closest of all research techniques to meeting the needs of fieldwork—it introduces no instrument between the fieldworker and the people he is studying, it permits the culture to be seen as a whole, and it permits the culture to be seen as the people themselves see it.

Participant-observation is primarily an indirect, unstructured procedure that is both an art and a science. As such it must always reflect the personality of the fieldworker and the receptivity of the people he studies. Some people hold even the skillful and resourceful fieldworker at arm's length, refusing to let him participate in more than the superficial aspects of their lives. Others induct the fieldworker into their daily lives, expecting that he will live as much like them as possible. Thus, while some anthropologists live for a year or more in the center of a village yet always remain isolated from its people and their inner lives, others enter a community so well that they sleep, eat, hunt, and make love as the local people do.

Not all fieldwork situations permit extensive participant-observation, and even under the most favorable circumstances the technique may have to be supplemented by other methods. For example, certain special incidents or historical occurrences may be understandable only through systematic interviewing; and various kinds of distributions or frequencies may call for systematic observation (Zelditch, 1962).

In the following sections, we will describe some of these methods and techniques and the value of the information that they can provide. These techniques can be divided roughly into two types. The first type we will discuss is intended for use with a limited number of persons. It includes the key-informant interview, the depth interview, ethnoscience, and the life history. These methods allow the anthropologist to probe deeply into certain areas of the culture; they are relatively unobtrusive and natural ways of collecting information. The second type is designed to gather a more representative kind of data from a larger number of persons. These methods include the genealogical method and census-taking which we have already discussed. In addition there are systematic observation, interviews of various kinds, questionnaires, psychological tests, and the making of various kinds of collections. These techniques permit measurement of variation among individuals as well as comparison between individuals or groups. After describing these methods we will discuss the technology that can be used with both types of methods.

Key-Informant Interviewing

As fieldwork progresses, the anthropologist discovers that some members of the community are better informants about their culture than others. Most anthropologists therefore come to rely upon certain persons for much of their detailed or specialized information. These people become what anthropologists call their *key informants*.

Often an anthropologist will find a native philosopher—an intelligent, articu-

A

KEY INFORMANTS. (a) Informant-interpreter, New Guinea Highlands (L. L. Langness). (b) Informant, Tanzania (R. B. Edgerton).

B

late, and knowledgeable person who has spent time reflecting on his culture and is willing to share his insights and generalizations with the anthropologist. Paul Radin (1927a) devoted an entire book to such persons, and many anthropologists have recorded their respect and indebtedness to persons like these who have helped them to understand the informant's culture.

Old people who no longer are sexually active are frequently a willing source of information about sexual behavior and beliefs, and they sometimes take great delight in telling an anthropologist what the rest of the adult community would be embarrassed or hesitant to discuss.

Some key informants are persons who have specialized knowledge that the rest of the community does not share—such as a child who knows current games and play, a woman with specialized knowledge of curing and herbs, or a sorcerer who is respected and feared in the community for his ability to *divine* and cast spells. Knowledge is power even in nonliterate communities, and practitioners may be unwilling to part freely with their information unless the anthropologist exchanges something for it, or somehow shows himself worthy, and earns the right to know.

Carlos Castaneda experienced this attitude in his relationship with the Yaqui man of knowledge, Don Juan. In his first book, Castaneda recounts how his struggles to learn through peyote convinced Don Juan that he was "chosen" to learn the secrets of a man of knowledge:

I have secrets I won't be able to reveal to anyone unless I find my chosen man. The other night when I saw you playing with Mescalito it was clear to me you were that man. But you are not an Indian. How baffling! (1968:30-31)

Castaneda's progress under the tutelage of Don Juan is a remarkable narrative about a special sort of key-informant relationship.

The first person who approaches the anthropologist offering to be a special friend and key informant is often someone the anthropologist should avoid—a person of low prestige or ability who seeks out the anthropologist solely in an effort to raise his own status in the community. Sometimes these persons of low status are also what are called marginal men. That is, for some reason, such as having been born in another area, they are not considered full members of the community. The marginal man in many societies is a person in a position to have unusual insight into the culture of the community. Nevertheless, in the early days of fieldwork the anthropologist is usually wiser to choose an influential person for the relationship of key informant.

The word *relationship* is important to emphasize because this kind of interviewing depends far more upon having a good personal relationship with the informant than it does upon a special program of interviewing tactics. Perhaps for this reason the informant is often a person of the same sex and about the same age as the anthropologist. By spending considerable time with such an informant, a relationship results which affects the fieldworker's social status in the community. He may become so strongly identified with the informant and his particular social groups—*clan*, faction, *lineage*, or *age-grade*—that he comes to "belong" to them and no amount of effort on his part will overcome the effects this affiliation has on other groups. Even so, there is much to recommend an influential key informant. Such persons can not only recall a wide range of events and explain most customs, but they are also likely to know more about how many important decisions were made and can influence other persons to make additional information available. They can also help the fieldworker in gaining access to ceremonies and important events.

For example, Norma Diamond's fieldwork in a village in Taiwan was facilitated by the sponsorship of influential members of the community. She was able to attend various activities at which women would ordinarily not be welcome. Discussing those opportunities, she says:

> On another occasion, I was invited to join the local Temple committee in an all-night meeting at which rituals for the well-being of the village were carried out. Again, women do not participate in this ceremony, nor do ordinary members of the village community. The ritual is performed by a closed group of hired priests and elected members of the Temple committee.
>
> In both instances, there were leading members of the community who thought it important that I be present if I were to understand local ways of doing things. My sex role then became neuter. (1970:127)

The key-informant relationship can involve considerable time on the part of the informant. In return, the fieldworker may offer payment or gifts. Reciprocity becomes part of the relationship but it should be carefully monitored so that the key informant does not misleadingly emphasize aspects of culture he knows the anthropologist to be interested in, ignoring others.

Because the key informant's view of the culture is just one person's view, complete with distortion arising from his own personal history, anthropologists rarely rely wholly upon one or a few key informants unless such persons represent the only living or available representatives of a culture that is no longer functioning or has been subjected to radical change. Instead, they utilize key-informant interviewing only as a supplement to their participant-observation and other techniques of fieldwork.

The Depth Inverview

There are subjects that rarely come up in normal conversation and there are other subjects that are sensitive and not easily discussed. Where strong emotions and deeply held values are involved, the fieldworker may resort to *depth interviewing* in which a confiding informant talks at length on a subject, allowing the investigator to probe deeply to reach what may be particularly difficult psychological information such as the informant's attitude toward Europeans, his relations with his parents or his children, or his involvement with witchcraft. Such interviews usually depend upon a key-informant relationship. They may also lead to life-history interviewing.

The Life History

The most intensive form of interviewing that is possible in fieldwork occurs when an anthropologist asks one of his key informants to tell him in detail the story of his life. This intensification and personalization of the ordinary key-informant relationship depends on strong rapport with an informant who is willing to give such a detailed account.

The technique is not an easy one to apply. If an informant is left to tell his story entirely his own way, the anthropologist has a cultural document which may be incomprehensible to persons outside the community. For example, Edward Winter's (1959) four life histories from Amba men and women in Uganda contain passages that are largely unintelligible without cultural interpretation. Linderman's life history of the Crow Indian, Plenty-coups, documents the efforts necessary to overcome this problem (1930).

Most nonliterate people are not introspective and do not spontaneously dictate their life histories. They seldom perceive the task in the same way that a person from the fieldworker's culture would. Thus, their accounts may not be chronological and may leave out expected information.

Fieldworkers usually guide the course of the life history with pertinent questions. Making up questions and determining when and where to ask them can often be delicate and as time-consuming as the actual interviewing. Problems of translation and interpretation can be extremely difficult. The anthropologist must be cautious not to put words into his informant's mouth. He must also be careful not to edit his information so drastically that its value is impaired. Above all the anthropologist must be patient and diligent.

The value of a life history goes beyond the value of specific information on events and customs of the past. In a life history, an individual comes together with the culture of his society in a unique way. One can see how cultural facts are organized in one individual's life span. One can also see the interplay between the individual and the culture; his life history may reveal both how the culture influenced him and his attitudes about various other aspects of culture and how much weight he gave such matters as religious beliefs and becoming a warrior. An informant's life history may also show how he influenced his culture. *Sun Chief* (Simmons, 1942), a life of a Hopi Indian, is a good example of this interplay.

The systematic use of life-history documents began in the United States among anthropologists working with American Indians. Paul Radin is often said to have been the most important figure in this development, and his autobiographical account of a Winnebago Indian, *Crashing Thunder* (1926), has been cited as the beginning of this type of work. The use of life histories has increased in recent years, in part due to the popularity and influence of the work of Oscar Lewis, which includes *The Children of Sanchez* (1961) and *Pedro Martinez* (1964).

Ethnoscience

Ethnoscientific techniques are a formal procedure designed to discover the different ways people perceive their world—hence the use of the prefix "ethno." The goal of an ethnoscientific description is to write a set of rules for a culture which is so complete that any outsider could use them to behave appropriately in that culture.

Most of the ethnoscience studies start with the assumption that the way people see and react to their world is significantly reflected in their language. For example, Americans have a set of terms for colors—*red*, *blue*, *yellow*, and the like. The Hanunóo of the Philippines, who were studied by Conklin (1955), see the world of color differently. Their set of terms considers not only color, but also the texture of the object at the same time. Thus, while the Hanunóo have only four basic color terms, these are associated with lightness, darkness, wetness, and dryness.

Ethnoscientists believe that they can find how the people classify their world by finding how they classify objects or events for which their language has terms. Working intensively with one or more key informants, the anthropologist starts with a "domain" or subject area within the native language, such as plants, diseases, or food. He then asks his informant for all the words that fall within that domain. If the domain were food, Americans might give him words such as *hot dog, hamburger, fruit, apple, banana, carrot, pie, cake*. Each of these terms falls under the general heading of *food*. The goal of the anthropologist is to discover how his informant classifies and sorts these terms into a taxonomy of food. He wants to know what characteristics an apple and a banana share that make Americans consider them to be members of the more general category fruit. He also wants to know what characteristics differentiate an apple and a banana from each other and from all other foods. How do Americans decide that an apple is not a banana or a hotdog or a piece of pie? From this information, the anthropologist can build both a system of classification and the rules for the classification.

An ethnoscientific study of disease was made among the Subanum of Indonesia (Frake, 1961). The goal was a logically arranged taxonomy of disease that reflected the Subanum way of thinking about disease. Within an area of culture, especially one such as disease where much specialized knowledge is involved, not all the Subanum can be expected to share the same classification system. Doctors may have a special way of looking at disease that the rest of the society does not have. This type of information is also of interest to the anthropologist. Understanding how people classify diseases may be important in understanding why doctors treat diseases in certain ways, why patients react to a diagnosis in other ways, and why some societies resist the introduction of Western medicine.

One of the complaints which has been leveled against the use of the ethnoscientific method is that it relies too much on an assumption that language classifications reflect categories of cognition, or how the people think, an assumption which has not yet been fully proven. The technique is obviously time-consuming and there are further criticisms that it has been used mainly to study "trivial" matters. This type of criticism reflects the past use of the technique, not the general goals of ethnoscience, nor the potential of the technique which can be used for important investigations. Begun in the late 1950's and developed in the 1960's, the ethnoscientific approach is still quite recent. It will probably become more useful when it is better integrated into general fieldwork so that its results can be seen in relationship to other pertinent information.

Systematic Observation

One drawback to participant-observation is the extent to which it depends upon the kind of events witnessed in the field situation and the personality of the individual anthropologist who reports them. How are others to evaluate what he reports as facts? Are they a probable truth or merely the personal opinion of one observer with whom others would disagree? *Systematic observational techniques* are rules for how to observe. These rules tell who, how, when, where, and what to look for and at, so that what one anthropologist reports from his observations will differ only minutely from what a fellow anthropologist (or anyone else trained by the same rules) would have observed in the same situation.

An anthropologist doing participant-observation in a camp of fierce, nomadic camel-raiders might watch the children at play and soon conclude in his notes, "Boys are more aggressive than the girls, here." He feels strongly convinced that his statement is true and several examples spring to mind. However, he wants to be more exact about just how aggressive the boys are, and he has in mind that he would like to compare them with boys in a peaceful farming community, where he also plans to do fieldwork. He now makes a series of systematic observations on children at play—observations made on random days, for specified periods of time, in which aggressive behaviors (which he has carefully defined so that anyone could recognize what he means) are carefully recorded in his notes of these observations. He can now be much more precise about the amount of aggression present, when it occurs most, and similar information. Furthermore, other anthropologists can see the type of data he used to reach his conclusions, and can use his techniques to gather comparable data in other societies.

CODE FOR CHILDREN'S BEHAVIOR

INDIVIDUAL BEHAVIORS

Individual Activities (IN) - Actions done by oneself which do not involve
participating with anyone else. Examples: imitation, eating, watching,
motor skills, individual play.

Chores (CH) - Tasks which are assigned to children as their share in the routine
of living. Individually done without direct instruction. Examples:
errands in homestead, cooking, tending fire, collecting wood, carrying
water, child care.

SOCIAL BEHAVIOR: MANDS (MANDS: ATTEMPTS TO CHANGE THE BEHAVIOR OF ANOTHER PERSON)

Sociable Mands (SM) - Attempting to initiate sociable interaction with another.
The subject may seek or offer sociability. Example: "Come and play
with me."

Egoistic Mands (EG) - Seeking behavior for the individual's own benefit. These
mands are divided into dependent (seeks comfort, help, material goods, etc.)
and dominant mands (seeks physical injury, seeks to annoy, seeks to take
property aggressively, etc.) (See below.)

Nurturant Mands (NU) - Offers help, comfort, etc., with the intent of meeting
the needs of another.

Pro-Social Mands (PS) - Mands whose intent is to make the respondent comply
to the needs of the group or homestead, or to the rules of etiquette
and behavior. Examples: mands re economic chores, mands re personal
hygiene, mands re child care. "Wash your hands for dinner." "Help
your brother put on his shoes."

Teaching Mands (TM) - Conscious attempts to transmit knowledge and skills
to P (the subject) using verbal means. Example: Giving out general
information or explaining a technique.

SOCIAL BEHAVIOR: OTHER

Social Play (PL) - Play with another individual or individuals.

Games (GA) - Social games with agreed upon rules such as football, or strategy
games such as marbles, stone pitching.

Sociability (SO) - Where the intention and content involves engaging in ongoing
friendly interaction. Examples: greetings, eats with, sings with, sits
with, is affectionate with.

Unintentional Behavior (UN) - Hurting another or oneself unintentionally.

<u>Detailed Code for Egoistic Mands</u> (Example)

Egoistic Dependent Mands

      01.   Seeks comfort
      02.   Seeks help
      03.   Seeks instrumental information (not for sociability)
      04a.   Seeks approval, praise, attention
      04b.   Seeks status acceptance
      05a.   Seeks material goods
      05b.   Seeks food
      06.   Seeks permission to do something for own pleasure or convenience

Egoistic Dominant Mands

      07.   Seeks physical injury; assaults, attempts to assault
      08.   Seeks to annoy, tease (when not for sociability)
      09.   Seeks to insult (more aggressive than EG08)
      10.   Seeks to take or destroy property aggressively
      11.   Seeks submission (pure dominance)
      12.   Seeks freedom from annoyance
      13.   Seeks competition
      14.   Other mands not clearly prosocial or nurturant
      15.   Seeks freedom from interaction

Other items included in overall coding of observations:

1.   Identification of all <u>personnel</u> in setting.
2.   <u>Location</u> of setting (house, yard, garden, etc.).
3.   Major <u>activities</u> occurring (housework, baby-sitting, play, etc.) involving the child.
4.   <u>Sequences</u> and continuity of related acts are identified in various ways. Example: (1) Mother asks child to do something, child ignores mother. (2) Mother asks again, child says "huh?" Child asks what mother wants, Mother says, "wash your hands."
5.   <u>Timing</u> of observational periods.

PRIMARY CODING CATEGORIES FOR CHILDREN'S SOCIAL BEHAVIOR. An illustration based on a code developed by Whiting *et al*. (1966), and adapted by Beatrice Whiting for field use by the Child Development Research Unit, University of Nairobi.

The anthropologist may also use systematic observations to check the accuracy of his informants' reports. Informants do not always do what they say or say what they do. For instance, a mother may report with great sincerity that she always picks her baby up when it cries. In fact, the anthropologist's observations may reveal that there are times, such as when her husband is home or she is in the middle of cooking, that she lets the baby cry for a long time before going to it. Some informants intend to mislead the anthropologist. Others are ashamed to admit the truth, and still others are merely unaware of what they actually are doing. It is therefore often a good idea for the anthropologist to doublecheck his informants' verbal statements with some systematic behavioral observations.

Beatrice and John Whiting are two anthropologists who have used systematic observation in large-scale projects in order to gather comparable data from a number of societies. One such project involved the systematic observation of child training in six cultures widely scattered throughout the world (B. Whiting, 1963). Other, more sophisticated projects are under way. Despite their commitment to this technique, the Whitings are among the first to recognize the tremendous expenditure in time and money required by such projects. Systematic observation requires preliminary study to determine what can be observed, and how. Then it requires training the observers to make sure they understand the rules that indicate what one looks for and how one knows if it has been seen. These observers may want to train local assistants who belong to the culture to perform the task with them. If an anthropologist were to attempt to duplicate all his data from participant-observation in this fashion, it could take a lifetime. The detailed observational techniques of Roger Barker and his colleagues (1963) illustrate the problems of making a narrative account of the behavior of even a single child, and Marvin Harris's (1964) equally detailed effort to objectively describe simple body motions provided ample evidence that such an approach, carried to its logical extreme, can become unreasonable when its results are seen in the light of the time and energy required to produce them.

Systematic Interviewing and Questionnaires

The anthropologist gathers much useful information from listening to and participating in conversations with various members of the community. At times, he may decide that he needs to supplement these conversations with more systematic data. Fieldworkers often recognize the need to ask similar questions of a large and representative sample of persons in the society. Many fieldworkers try to avoid formal procedures in which a standard set of questions is asked under specified conditions. They feel that standardized questions may be misinterpreted so that the answers given may not refer to the question that the anthropologist thought he was asking. The answers are then not useful or comparable. These are important considerations to the anthropologist who hopes to get the insider's point of view.

FIELD OBSERVATION PROTOCOL

NAME __Charles__   SEX __1__   AGE __8__   DATE __21-8-72__

HOMESTEAD & ID __17208__   OBSERVER __Name__   TIME ELAPSED __30 mins.__

Time	Personnel Sequence	Activity	Location/Act Act #	Behavior Code
12:30 12:31	S-17208 O-17207 17209 17202	P. TALKS WITH JOHN AND GEOF ABOUT PLAYING FOOTBALL	01	Yard SO 02
	S-17208 O-17207 S1	P. AND JOHN START PULLING EACH OTHER AND LAUGHING	02	PL 00
12:32	S-17202 O- 17208 17207 S9	MA TELLS THEM TO BE CAREFUL NOT TO HURT PAT	03	ST 01 PS 03 C 01
	S-17208 O-17207 S1	P. AND JOHN CONTINUE TALKING. P. ASKS JOHN TO COME WITH HIM. JOHN COMPLIES	04	SM 08 C 01
12:33	S-17208 17207 O-17202 S9	P. AND JOHN PICK UP SOME LEAVES AND TALK TO MA ABOUT THEM. MA C.	05	ST 01 EG 03 C 01
12:34	S-17208 O-17209	P. ASKS GEOF FOR SUGAR CANE TO EAT. GEOF C.	06	EG 052 C 1
	S-17208 O-17207 S1	P. TELLS JOHN TO TAKE SOAP	07	ST 01 NC 14 PS 01 CH 01
	S-17202 O-17208 S9	MA SAYS NO	08	ST 02 EG 11
	S-17202 O-17208	MA TELLS P. TO GET THE BASKET. P. DOES NOT HEAR	09	PS 01 C 07
12:35	S-17208	P. STANDS NEAR OBA FIDDLING WITH STICK AND STANDS AROUND	10	IN 00
12:36	S-17208 O-17206	P. ASKS PETER TO PLAY FOOTBALL PETER SAYS NOTHING	11	ST 01 SM 08 NC 06
	S-17208 O-00082	P. RUNS AFTER A SHEEP AND HITS HER	12	EG 07 ST 09 NC 19
	O-99991 S-17208 S1	JOHN AND THE KIDS TELL P. THEY ARE GOING	13	SO 01
12:37	S-17208 S2	P. LOOKS AFTER THEM AS THEY MOVE DOWN THE PATH	14	IN 11
	S-17208 O-17207 S9	P. TELLS JOHN TO WAIT FOR HIM. JOHN KEEPS WALKING	15	SM 08 ST 01 NC 6

Notes: S = subject of act; P. = child being observed; O = object of act;
Ma = Mother of P.; C. = complies (to a mand); NC - non-compliance; ST = style or
way in which an act is done by subject; S1...S9 = sequencing of behaviors.

A WRITTEN NARRATIVE PROTOCOL AS SUBSEQUENTLY AMPLIFIED. This is from a study by Thomas S. Weisner of rural-urban differences in Kenyan children's social behavior. These children were in their rural homestead during observation; they have also been observed while living in Nairobi. The division into enumerated acts and the various codings were added after the observation. (Based on procedures developed by John and Beatrice Whiting for the Child Development Research Unit, University of Nairobi)

Furthermore, a formal interview situation is often stiff and awkward, leading to reluctance, deception, or misunderstanding. Imagine yourself being "interviewed"; then imagine yourself simply having a discussion with a neighbor or visitor. The differences are obvious.

For all of these reasons, fieldworkers often prefer to use an informal approach to interviewing in which they have a set of topics that they try to introduce during natural conversations. They may ask about a topic in many different ways until they are certain that they are not being misunderstood and are getting the kind of information they are seeking. Asking the same question on various occasions throughout the fieldwork, on the assumption that not everyone will be able to lie consistently, is another technique for checking the accuracy of answers or guarding against the possibility of deception.

A somewhat more formal variant of interviewing, which also aims at maintaining the integrity of the informant's point of view, is the open-end interview. The anthropologist asks a very general question and then permits the informant to talk at length, elaborating, volunteering, and pursuing whatever is of interest to him. Although this form of interviewing does have some structure to it, it is still more like a conversation than a systematically organized set of questions such as typically constitutes an "interview." For example, one might ask, "What is the most important thing that can happen to someone in life?" Or, "What do you think is the biggest difference between men and women?" Edgerton (1971) asked questions of this kind of more than 500 persons in four East African societies, and the answers given were typically both thoughtful and revealing.

All of the interviewing techniques discussed thus far have the same basic strengths and weaknesses. They are used in fieldwork because they are relatively flexible and personal, and they permit the anthropologist to achieve an "insider's" understanding of the culture. They also allow the anthropologist to be "natural" by asking questions only of those people (such as his key informants) with whom he already has good relations. The weaknesses lie in the fact that information collected in this way may not be *representative*, and often cannot be quantified or replicated by other anthropologists. Many anthropologists believe that participant-observation often permits them to know whether the information collected through interviews is true or not. Most believe, however, that not even the most prolonged and intensive participant-observation can always provide such assurances. It is to acquire new information or to clarify some existing doubt that interviews are conducted in the first place. But if an interview is carried out with only one or two informants, how is one to know whether the information is representative of others in the community? Or if one does ask many persons but uses an unsystematic procedure, how is one to repeat it?

These problems lead some anthropologists to turn to systematic or "survey" inteviewing of the kind used in assessing "public opinion" or voter preference. The Gallup Poll is a well-known example. The Kinsey report on sexual behavior is another. This kind of interviewing attempts to assure representativeness by

106. "When you hear someone say that a person is "mentally ill," what does that mean to you?"
_____

107. "As far as you know, what is a nervous breakdown?"
_____

108. "As far as you know, how does a psychiatrist go about helping the people who go to him?"
_____

109. "As far as you know does a psychiatrist really help the people who go to him?"

(0)____No   (1)____Yes   (2)____Other   (SPECIFY)_____
_____

110. "Do you personally know anyone who you think would be helped if they would see a psychiatrist?"

(0)____No   (1)____Yes   (VOLUNTARY ELABORATION)_____
_____
_____

"Now I am going to read you some statements and I will ask you if you agree or disagree with each one."

(USE ONLY ONE RESPONSE FOR EACH STATEMENT)	NO	YES	UNDECIDED
111. "Most mental illness is curable."	0	1	2
112. "If the circumstances were bad enough, anyone could become mentally ill."	0	1	2
113. "Mental illness can arise from lack of will-power"	0	1	2
114. "Mental illness may be brought on as a punishment for sins."	0	1	2
115. "Most mental illness comes from tensions and troubles in the family."	0	1	2
116. "A nervous breakdown will grow into insanity if help is not given."	0	1	2
117. "Mental illness is often inherited."	0	1	2
118. "Prayer is the best answer when one is very nervous and worried."	0	1	2
119. "Mental disorders have their beginnings in childhood."	0	1	2
120. "A person who has a nervous breakdown can recover faster if he is with his family."	0	1	2

PART OF AN INTERVIEW SCHEDULE. Developed by R. B. Edgerton and Marvin Karno for the study of mental illness. Categories "0", "1", and "2" are provided to assist computer processing of the responses. These numbers are commonly used on punch cards and in statistical processing. The interviewer records the actual words given in answers to some questions (example, 107); but for others (examples, 111-120) the interviewer only circles the number corresponding to the answer given.

sampling. To sample, one first must specify the entire population—known as the ''universe''—with which one is concerned. Then one selects a subpopulation, a ''sample,'' of the universe by some technique that permits one to know in what ways the sample represents the larger population. Members of the sample may be chosen by selecting categories of people—old, wealthy, female, or the like. Or they may be chosen by a probability technique that gives each person in the population the same probability of falling into the sample. Sampling techniques can become very complex as populations become large, stratified, mobile, or the like. These problems are discussed further in Part III.

Survey interviewing makes replication possible, at least in principle, by rigorously standardizing the questions asked, the order in which they are asked, the manner of the interviewer, the place of interview, and other relevant factors. Despite obstacles to such standardization in many non-Western communities (people wander out in the middle of an interview, animals and babies wander in, an unwanted audience often gathers, or everyone suddenly leaves to drink beer), some anthropologists have been successful in standardizing their interviewing procedures and thereby, presumably, increasing the comparability of the information they receive. The same procedures make it possible to quantify the answers in a meaningful way. If many people, whose representativeness is known, are all asked the same questions, in the same ways, then it may be reasonable to count and compare their answers.

What this kind of interviewing achieves in its precision, it loses elsewhere. It makes little sense to present a question in exactly the same way to large numbers of people if those people do not fully understand the question or are not willing to answer it. For this reason, anthropologists usually confine their use of survey interviewing to matters that most people can easily understand and are willing to discuss. As we have already mentioned, census information can sometimes be elicited by survey interviewing; so can certain kinds of economic information, beliefs about what is true or proper, attitudes toward health and disease, and the like.

Questionnaires differ from survey interviews in their reliance upon writing. The questions are written, then mailed or delivered to the persons in the sample. The answers are written, then mailed back or picked up. When one wishes to reach a very large number of persons the questionnaire can be useful. Its specific weaknesses are its dependency upon literacy and the difficulty in assuring that people write their answers and return them. Questionnaires are generally not useful in small nonliterate communities. Although anthropologists have sometimes used this technique of eliciting information, they have usually done so when their work is in cities, or when they are attempting to contact knowledgeable persons (government officers, medical personnel, migrant laborers, school children) who are not resident in the community they are studying. Lewis Henry Morgan used questionnaires in this way as early as 1858, sending them to a number of Indian agents and missionaries to elicit information on kinship systems. Later he sent hundreds of such questionnaires throughout the world and was able to compile a massive amount of information on kinship systems which he incorporated into his famous book *Systems of Consanguinity and Affinity of the Human Family* (1870).

Because anthropologists are being forced to abandon their rapidly disappearing small-scale societies and to work more and more in urban and large-scale societies, many of them have shifted their reliance to more formal sampling procedures and to survey interviewing, testing, or questionnaires. An equal number, however, continue to feel that even in the largest urban setting there is an important place for intensive and personal participant-observation and for the kind of understanding that only this technique can provide. There are examples of the successful use of traditional participant-observation in modern urban communities; examples are in Liebow's (1967) study of a black ghetto community, Keiser's (1969) work with a teenage gang, or Banton's (1957) study of a West African city.

Psychological Tests

The effect of a culture in shaping the personality, cognition, and perception of its members is a topic which has long interested anthropologists. Anthropologists have often used psychological tests in fieldwork to probe for psychological material which is difficult to reach in other ways. Such material has been used to study the extent to which culture molds the personalities of its members into similar shapes; it has been used to compare personality types of one culture with another; it has also been used to determine whether or not there is a typical psychological ''set'' with which persons of a certain culture face the world—a pattern of expectations, attitudes and fears which guide their reactions to events.

Unfortunately, many of the tests which anthropologists might use are too *culture-bound* (relevant for one culture only) to be useful in another culture or for purposes of making comparisons between two cultures. Standard intelligence tests are examples of culture-bound tests, since these tests require a background of experiences and information which non-Westerners do not share. Invariably but hardly surprisingly, when such tests have been used, they have demonstrated the ''inferiority'' of the non-Westerners taking them. This is a serious matter in the United States, too, where ethnic minorities with a background of experience within a different subculture do not do as well as middle-class whites. For this reason anthropologists (Brace, *et al.*, 1972) have been severely critical of recent claims by various psychologists such as Jensen (1969) and Eysenck (1971) that American blacks have lower average intelligence scores than whites because of a different genetic inheritance rather than a different cultural inheritance.

Because of the culture-bound nature of many tests, the psychological tests used

A

EXAMPLES OF PROJECTIVE TESTS. (a) Card 12F from the Murray Thematic Apperception Test. This is an example of an ambiguous projective stimulus used to evoke hidden fantasy material. Anthropologists have often redrawn these standard TAT cards for use in other cultures. (Copyright 1943, 1971) (b) This is an example from the Goldschmidt-Edgerton picture technique for studying values. Here the picture is less ambiguous than those in the Murray tests, portraying a more-or-less clear-cut scene of potential conflict. This card, used among the Pokot of Kenya, was intended to evoke values and attitudes relating to sexuality, especially adultery. (Edgerton, 1971)

B

by anthropologists have usually been the so-called *projective tests*. These are tests that present persons with an ambiguous stimulus, such as an ink-blot. The person's response is less likely to be due to the properties of the stimulus or what he knows about it because he has not met such a thing before in his experience. It is believed that what he reads into the ink-blot comes (is "projected") from himself and reflects his personality. Such tests as the Rorschach Ink-Blot Test, the Thematic Apperception Test (TAT) and the Draw-a-Man-Test were developed for clinical use, but have been widely employed in fieldwork for many years.

While some of these tests, such as the Rorschach, require specialized training to use, others such as sentence completion or various versions of the TAT can be easily modified for use in the field. Even these tests do not completely escape the cultural stamp of their makers, and when not used with care may lead to far-fetched misinterpretations of other cultures based upon the assumption that a certain response means the same thing both in a non-Western society and in ours. Thus, while anthropologists continue to use these tests, debate continues over their value as cross-culturally valid ways of understanding people and their culture.

There is continuing evidence that people from different cultures have slightly different perceptual abilities as well as different styles of perceiving and thinking about their world. Colin Turnbull's experience with his Pygmy friend Kenge is an example (1961:262). Kenge, who had previously never been far from the thickly wooded Ituri Forest, was taken by Turnbull to a high promontory which over-looked a vast plain on which buffalo were grazing. The Pygmy, who was not acquainted with what distance can do to the apparent size of objects, insisted that the buffalo were "insects." In fact, he refused to believe otherwise. Turnbull then drove Kenge nearer and nearer to the "insects" until they became recognizable to him as buffalo at least twice the size of the smaller buffalo that inhabit the Ituri Forest. Kenge was so transfixed and awed by the change that he was speechless.

Anthropologists have long been intrigued by the notion that differences in the way that people perceive and think about their world may be due to their cultural experiences, and quite a few fieldworkers have investigated this problem using a range of psychological tests. There are perceptual tests of optical illusions, like the Müller-Lyer test (of the apparent differences in length of two equally long lines), or tests of the relative size of objects seen at a distance, or of the ability to perceive a human or animal figure that is embedded in a camouflaging background. Other tests have been devised to determine people's ability to remember certain familiar or unfamiliar things, or to count, or to identify and recall colors, or to solve various sorts of practical or abstract problems.

The importance of these tests for anthropologists lies in the possibility that differences in perceptual ability are produced by specific aspects of people's physical and cultural environment. For example, studies have been made to determine whether people who live in round houses perceive things differently from people who live in rectangular houses. Robbins (1966) reports that people who live in circular houses prefer straight-line figures in their art styles, whereas those with rectangular houses prefer curved figures. And Segall, Campbell, and Herskovits (1966) report that people who live in rectangular houses perceive A in the Müller-Lyer illusion as being shorter than B. It is not yet known why these differences occur.

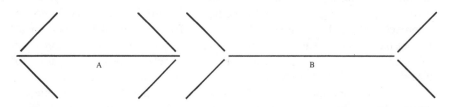

THE MÜLLER-LYER ILLUSION. Lines A and B are of equal length.

The results of psychological tests such as these pose intriguing questions just as they offer important insights. Unfortunately, they have all the disadvantages of survey interviewing, since they must be presented in a standardized manner, plus the additional disadvantage of asking people to perform a task which is totally foreign to them. For this reason some anthropologists avoid these tests, fearing that the results will be misleading, while at the same time the use of the tests risks the loss of their carefully won rapport within the community.

ROUND HOUSES. These contrast with the rectilinear houses in the ''carpentered'' world of the West. (R. B. Edgerton)

Making Collections

The cultural patterns of a people can be seen in more than just their verbalizations or the ways they behave. They are also reflected in the objects that they create. The earliest anthropologists made extensive collections of all kinds of material culture—tools, weapons, ornaments, clothing, musical instruments, artistic products, pottery, even entire dwellings or ocean-going boats. Money from museum sources provided much of the impetus for these collections and as a result museums became filled with material things from all parts of the world. The anthropologists of the time were concerned with questions of creativity, but they were also interested in material culture as evidence of stages of evolution, and in the possibility of tracing historical connections and *diffusion* between societies on the basis of similarities in their material products.

As interest in these questions died out, "mere collecting" came to be denigrated. Modern fieldworkers tend to limit their collections to such things as medicinal plants, which are carefully preserved for later chemical analysis in laboratories, or the seeds of food plants (which are analyzed for genetic structure and probable historical origin). Many fieldworkers have ignored material culture except for its most obvious military, economic, or religious significance. Thus, when earlier anthropologists did fieldwork among the Australian Aborigines, for whom day-to-day survival depends upon the proper use of tools and weapons, they wrote at length about spears, stone tools, throwing sticks, and other essential aspects of their technology. But when the influential A. R. Radcliffe-Brown was doing fieldwork with Australian Aborigines shortly after the turn of the century, he had no interest whatever in material culture, being concerned only with the functional analysis of kinship and marriage. The Australian anthropologist C. W. M. Hart reports that when he went to study the Tiwi of Northern Australia in 1928,

Technology bored me. All the young functionalists of those early days had a profound contempt for the type of anthropology book that contained dozens of pages of descriptions of how the people made pots or baskets or cut digging sticks, a contempt which Radcliffe-Brown (and later, after I left the Tiwi, Malinowski) did much to encourage. (1970:157)

American anthropologists of that same period still had some interest in material culture (and obligations to museums who supported their fieldwork), but in America too, cultural anthropology diverted its attention from material culture to other aspects of culture more theoretically relevant or more fashionable. As a result, comparative studies of material culture have been until very recently almost nonexistent. Wendell Oswalt (1973:vii), who has recently attempted an integrated cross-cultural study of technology, has referred to the prior neglect of the subject as "surprising, startling, perplexing, annoying, aggravating, virtually incomprehensible."

As Oswalt points out, human survival and human culture itself are dependent upon man's ability to manufacture things. Archaeologists study things—artifacts as they are usually called—almost exclusively, and their success in reconstructing culture from artifacts has been impressive. But modern cultural anthropologists continue to pay little attention to the ways in which the people they study make and use things, perhaps because so much of the "original" technology has been lost, and replaced by "uninteresting" or familiar artifacts of Western origin. This neglect is apparent in most textbooks, where material culture receives only passing mention before the introduction of subjects such as energetics, economy, or ecology—all of which are inseparable from technology. A recent text by Philip Bock (1969) is a rare exception.

It seems evident that fieldwork methods should include careful study of how people make and use material things. The way an object is made and the reasons and choices that underlie its manufacture can provide useful information about a people's knowledge of physical principles. The uses of an object and patterns of sharing it may reveal much about social relations. Aesthetic details in the manufacture of an object may reflect social arrangements in the society, social changes, and important social themes, as well as aspects of the psychology of the people who made it. In this regard, Thomas Gladwin's (1970) study of Polynesian navigators provides an insight into these people's knowledge of physical laws concerning hull shape, sail size, wave flow, tides, winds, astronomy, and the like.

Even in societies where Western technology has become dominant it is important to see how material forms may be used for subsistence, for aesthetic or medical purposes, or simply for recreation. The study of material things may tell us a great deal about the functioning of various aspects of a culture; the study of how material things which have been borrowed from other societies are modified to fit into a new society may be even more revealing.

Archaeologists have begun to study living peoples to gain a better understanding of the artifacts such peoples leave behind (Gould, 1969). It is possible that ethnographers will reverse this process, and attempt to sharpen their methods of studying living peoples by learning more about the artifacts they make, someday to leave behind.

Technological Aids to Fieldwork

Modern technology has placed in the hands of the anthropologist several ways to capture the ongoing stream of events in a society, to stop time in effect, and to preserve these events for later examination. With tools such as camera, tape-recorder, and cinematic film, the anthropologist need not rely merely on his memory of an event. He can produce it for others to study so that they may judge the accuracy of his observations or make comparisons with other societies. He may also return to it himself repeatedly for detailed analysis of more subtle aspects of behavior or to seek important explanatory variables that he may have overlooked while watching the event actually take place.

The tape-recorder can now capture what used to be laboriously taken down by hand such as verbatim accounts of conversation or folktales. Folklore, including everything from jokes, riddles, songs, and children's stories to myths of the origin of the people, or other sacred stories, can be important in understanding a people's past (by comparison with the folklore of other cultures), or their present (by analyzing the attitudes and values that these tales embody).

The tape-recorder can also be used by members of the culture themselves, as, for example, when mothers cooperate to gather material for the anthropologist on their children's natural speech patterns in the home. Material which is gathered can then be played back to members of the culture for comment and explanation where necessary.

The use of a tape-recorder allows speech to occur at its natural pace, gives a more accurate and complete version of the speech events, and often seems less obtrusive than note-taking, especially after the speakers have become used to the idea of a recorder, although the extent to which speakers who know they are being recorded return to natural speech is still open to debate. Oscar Lewis used the tape-recorder to gather all the day-to-day interactions of the persons he studied from which he edited the material for his widely acclaimed books about Mexico and Puerto Rico. In these books, the people convey the flavor of their days and the meaning of life for them in their own words, with an immediacy and authenticity that can only be experienced.

The following passage is a remembrance by Esperanza of her wedding night with Pedro Martinez more than thirty years earlier:

I was terribly afraid. . . . Chills came over me. I was terribly afraid, for never, never had we spoken to one another. After we ate dinner Pedro's aunt went to bed and so did he. He had gone to bed with his clothes on. He has always done that. I also always go to bed with my clothes on. The aunt told me that for this I had got married and that I should go to bed. I was very afraid and ashamed. Pedro covered me with the blanket and then began to embrace me and fondle my breasts. Then he went on top of me. I didn't know what the men did to one, and I said to myself, "maybe it's like this." I felt like crying or going to my mother, but I remembered that they had married me and then I said, "if I die, I'll die. I have to go through it here even though he kills me." And I closed my eyes and waited for the worst. (Lewis, 1959:40)

If one could not record her words exactly, could her emotions ever be captured adequately?

The use of photography in fieldwork deserves special mention. The popularity of photography in fieldwork has grown to such an extent that books have been written on "visual anthropology" (Collier, 1967), and universities have developed programs in "ethnographic film." Of course, the use of still photography as a means of illustrating material culture, landscape, or personal appearance is almost as old as ethnography. However, it was not until Mead and Bateson's trip to Bali (1942) that photography was used as a central means of collecting data in fieldwork. Similarly, although Flaherty's famous film *Nanook of the North* was made in 1922, the use of cinematography in fieldwork was rare before the 1950's.

Since the 1950's, anthropologists have been experimenting with all forms of photography in recording cultural events. This growth in the use of photography is due in part to the fact that cameras and film have become better and less expensive, and in part to innovations such as portable video-tape cameras with instant replay capability.

Anthropologists today may use film to help them make a proxemic analysis—an analysis of the cultural meaning of the way persons locate themselves in space for social interactions. Body language is a popular way of referring to the same thing. In similar fashion they may use their film for finely detailed studies of the cultural repertoire of facial expressions and ways of touching, or the interactions between a mother and child.

Certain events that are particularly rare, complex, or important may receive special attention. *Event analysis* involves making as complete a record as possible (involving the combined use of photography, tape-recording, interviewing, and participant-observation) of a two- or three-day event. Such events would typically include initiation ceremonies, religious rituals, economic transactions, births, funerals, and marriages (Goldschmidt, 1972).

Anthropologists may use all forms of photography to record a variety of cultural aspects. They take extensive film footage of ceremonies, everyday village life, economic practices, warfare, and virtually everything else you might think of. Some anthropologists give easy-to-operate Super-8 cameras to members of a community and ask them to film whatever they wish. The results may reveal insights into what members of that community consider to be important. In this sense they are comparable to the biographies discussed in the life history section.

The current interest in various technological aids to fieldwork has been growing and is likely to continue to grow as anthropologists incorporate their use into the existing repertoire of techniques, devise new ways to study old problems, or explore film and tapes as techniques in and of themselves for presenting cultural data. Technological aids can provide a better way to record certain aspects of the native way of life. They cannot replace the anthropologist, however, for without his understandings, the ongoing action remains incomprehensible to outsiders, with the reasons and the meanings behind social gestures obscured from all but the actors themselves. We shall discuss such techniques in the presentation of ethnographic data in Part II.

Leaving the Field

The day finally comes when the anthropologist must prepare for his departure home. If he found a contented existence and good friends in the group he lived with, saying goodbye to people whom he may not see again for many years, perhaps never, is difficult:

"When you go," Maiamuta, the headman of Tofmora, said to me once, "it will be as if you died. I will cut off my finger and cover my head with dirt. Then I will burn your house so I do not have to see it every day." Though he spoke figuratively, I will not believe that he chose his words only for effect. He was ill on the day of my departure, and I said good-by to him in his house, kneeling to look at him where he lay on the ground in the semidarkness. As I walked away, someone told me that he had pulled himself to the door of the hut and called to me. . . . (Read, 1965:8)

But even if the anthropologist is relieved to be going and anxious to return home, he must nevertheless do what he can to leave the area open to other fieldworkers who may follow.

Many anthropologists have a continuing and meaningful relationship with the people they lived among and studied. Anthropologists have sometimes attempted to train members of the community to continue collection of data for them, mailing instructions and data back and forth. More often, though, the relationship has been one of continuing the friendships through correspondence, helping out when needed, even entertaining members of the community who may come to visit the anthropologist's country. The day may also come when the anthropologist returns to visit or work with his group, to chronicle the changes that have taken place in the lives of its members since he lived with them.

Even if the anthropologist were never again to speak to any member of the community, he would not escape a moral linkage to them forged by his act of doing fieldwork and writing about it, for some of its members may someday read what he has written, or in a non-literate community, their sons may someday read it and approve, or be hurt, quarrel, or rejoice, or perhaps even learn facts about a past now forgotten by most. In this way fieldwork can have a direct impact on the members of the culture described. Others with power over the community may also read about the culture and on the basis of what they read, make decisions and take actions which will change lives in the community. What has been written will become part of the community's public reputation and for this reason the anthropologist faces the problem of presenting his data in a way which will fulfill the needs of scientific accuracy yet also fulfill his moral obligations to the people he worked with and who shared their lives with him.

As he leaves the field, the anthropologist's mind is often less on what he will be writing than it is on his homecoming. Anthropologist Alan Beals, returning from a long period of fieldwork in the Indian village of Gopalpur, confessed, "We thought of rare beef steak, shower baths, and the joys of being once again among people we could really understand" (1970:55). The reality of the return home and the adjustment back to one's own culture may, however, produce culture shock in reverse. Beals goes on to chronicle his feelings as he and his wife and child once again actually settled into life back home:

. . .The baby took one look at her grandmother and burst into tears. We could not understand why people were so distant, so hard to reach, or why they talked and moved so quickly. We were a little frightened at the sight of so many white faces and we could not understand why no one stared at us, brushed against us, or admired our baby. . . . We had returned to civilization. We were suffering from culture shock. In time we would get used to it. We would never forget that once we lived in a world that had not yet gone mad. (1970:55)

Before long, the shock will fade and everything will be familiar once again. Before this happens, blurring the once vivid memories of the field experience, the anthropologist is wise to immerse himself in the task of organizing and analyzing his field data. Not only must the returned fieldworker do everything he can to retain his knowledge of the strange cultural world he has just left, he must begin the task of presenting what he has learned to others.

Further Readings

Students who are interested in a more advanced and detailed discussion of the methods and issues of fieldwork should read P. J. Pelto, *Anthropological Research* (1970). A more highly advanced but nevertheless excellent treatment of the same subjects, as well as others, is available in Raoul Naroll and Ronald Cohen, *Handbook of Method in Cultural Anthropology* (1970).

Students may also wish to pursue further certain specialized aspects of fieldwork. We recommend, for example, W. J. Filstead, *Qualitative Methodology* (1970), for a review of many of the issues of fieldwork as they spill over into other social sciences, and E. Webb, *et al.*, *Unobtrusive Measures* (1966) for a discussion of research techniques that do not alter the behavior of the people being studied. The more practical problems of fieldwork are well introduced by T. R. Williams, *Field Methods in the Study of Culture* (1967). A related essay is D. Nash, "The Ethnologist as Stranger" (1963). The following titles will also prove helpful to students interested in more detailed treatments: E. L. Schusky, *Manual for Kinship Analysis* (1965), J. Collier, Jr., *Visual Anthropology* (1967), S. C. Gudschinsky, *How to Learn an Unwritten Language* (1967), S. A. Richardson, *et al.*, *Interviewing* (1965), and Beatrice and John Whiting, "Methods for Observing and Recording Behavior" (1970).

An excellent source of information about the experience and methods of fieldwork is a number of recently published personal accounts of fieldwork by anthropologists. Students will find the following books to be not only highly informative, but entertaining as well: Joseph B. Casagrande, *In the Company of Man* (1960), M. Freilich, *Marginal Natives* (1970), Peggy Golde, *Women in the Field* (1970), F. Henry and S. Saberwal, *Stress and Response in Fieldwork* (1969), Solon T. Kimball and James B. Watson, *Crossing Cultural Boundaries* (1972), Hortense Powdermaker, *Stranger and Friend* (1966), G. D. Spindler, *Being an Anthropologist* (1970), and Rosalie Wax, *Doing Fieldwork* (1971).

PART II STYLES: PRESENTING ETHNOGRAPHIC INFORMATION

The same care and hard work that goes into fieldwork is required when the anthropologist sits down to write a description of the culture he or she has just finished studying. These two tasks are of equal importance for anthropology, yet almost exclusive attention has been given to fieldwork methods, and there has been a corresponding neglect of the techniques of presentation. This difference can be seen clearly (and unfortunately) in the fact that many courses in field techniques and methods are offered and required in Departments of Anthropology, but there are virtually none in writing of any kind. Yet the anthropologist may be the only outside observer who knows the cultural pattern of the society in which he has worked. Therefore accuracy in recapturing his experiences is a serious intellectual commitment and the styles used to present ethnographic information become an important topic for consideration.

In this section, we will discuss the important task of presenting ethnographic information. We shall first describe the usual ways in which anthropologists communicate ethnographic information to their colleagues in order to add to a fund of general knowledge about other cultures. We shall also compare these professional presentations with similar efforts by nonanthropologists. We shall then examine other styles of presentation which treat cultural data in a different mode, and we will discuss why these alternate styles have developed and how they can complement the more standard style of presentation.

The Standard Style of Scientific Ethnography

Analyzing field data and writing research reports are hard work; few anthropologists actually enjoy either. But without this hard, lonely, undramatic work, anthropological knowledge would not be effectively disseminated, and our understanding of human beings and culture could not accumulate and improve.

57

The anthropologist, newly returned from doing fieldwork, faces a massive job of organization before he can even begin to write. A typical fieldworker returns with boxes, trunks, and crates full of notes, tapes, films, and specimens of material culture. These must be reduced to order, and then filed. The anthropologist must sort, classify, count, separate, and "make sense out of" masses of field notes, forms, tests, interviews, censuses, and genealogies, which relate to matters such as marriage, kinship, economics, court cases, divorce, religion, witchcraft, and social relations.

This process inevitably entails *generalization*. During the fieldwork itself, the anthropologist notices and records some things while ignoring others. He does so, as we have seen, because of his personality, his training, and his theoretical interests. In all fieldwork, the reality of the stream of human behavior is condensed and to some degree is altered. Some behaviors are classed together; others are separated because they are considered dissimilar. This process of classifying things as similar or different is another aspect of generalization. So is the process of categorizing behavior as "aggression," "marriage," or "happiness." Even if these categories accurately describe the behavior being seen, they are no more than shorthand summaries for the behavior or the emotion involved.

The process of generalization is central to what the anthropologist does in fieldwork. It becomes even more central when he writes his ethnographic description. Generalization is dictated only in part by the practical necessity to reduce the realities of the cultural world to a limited number of publishable pages. The most important reason for generalization is dictated by the nature of the cultural code which the anthropologist is attempting to describe. The cultural code which underlies behavior in a society may be likened in part to a grammar which underlies the speech of the society. The linguist does not describe a culture's rules of language by simply writing down every speech event he hears and the context in which it occurred; nor does the anthropologist describe the society's cultural patterns by setting forth every episode he witnessed and every conversation he had. Human beings in all communities abstract, classify, and generalize—and it is precisely such generalized understandings which make up their cultural code. To describe this set of generalized understandings is one of the major goals of anthropologists.

Generalization, either as a necessary summarization or as the search for a people's underlying codes, rules, or abstractions, need not lead to inaccuracy. A summary can be just as accurate as the more complete reality that it condenses. But it can also be inaccurate if it omits, overemphasizes, or distorts the reality that it attempts to represent. Robert Lowie discussed the problem this way:

At times ethnography shares its subject matter with literature but its attitude is distinct. An exotic milieu, say, Tahiti, impresses itself on the sensibilities of a Pierre Loti, whose talent may convey similar thrills to the reader. An ethnographer does less and more. He renounces aesthetic impressions except as a by-product; he does not select his facts for literary effectiveness since his duty lies in depicting the whole of cultural reality. As a naturalist cannot confine himself to beautiful butterflies, so the ethnographer must ignore nothing that belongs to social tradition. He records a boys' game on stilts as faithfully as he does the cosmogonies of Tahitian priests: both are part of his theme, and children at play may reveal as much of basic cultural process as does the metaphysical speculation of their elders. (Lowie, 1937:3-4)

Franz Boas published 5000 pages of ethnography about the Kwakiutl Indians of the Pacific Northwest. But even this enormous amount of writing was not sufficient to give an adequate basis for a general understanding of Kwakiutl culture, because Boas was too selective, omitting certain kinds of crucial materials while overemphasizing others (Codere, 1957).

The primary goal in ethnographic writing, as in fieldwork itself, is accuracy —providing a true account of a people's culture. In many sciences, the rules of experimental procedure can be easily stated so that any other scientist can understand just what was done and can duplicate the research if he wishes. Thus accuracy is assessed by repeating the procedure and finding the same result. Precise and simple field methods are foreign to fieldwork, and accuracy cannot be determined by repeating the fieldwork. Nevertheless, in preparing an ethnographic report, the anthropologist should specify his field methods in sufficient detail to let the reader judge how well he controlled bias, how he obtained the data that he reports, what he might have missed, and perhaps even why he missed it.

If the ethnographic writer takes this charge seriously, then he must provide readers with a substantial amount of information about how fieldwork was conducted and about any important variables that might have had an impact on the culture itself. What were the historical events that could significantly have come into play? What were the current political conditions? How was the fieldworker initially received? How did his role and rapport change over time? How well did he speak the language? How good were his interpreters? How much of the culture did he have access to? What aspects of the culture were not accessible? Under what conditions were certain kinds of data collected? If specialized techniques (of interview, testing, or observation) were employed, what were the details of their use? What theories or problems guided the fieldwork and, possibly, distorted it? Did personal bias become a factor in the research? Did illness or injury play any part in what the fieldworker did or saw? These questions are only a sample of the kind of questions that should be answered in order to let the reader judge how well the research was done and whether, in principle if not in actuality, the research would lead to the same findings if it were repeated.

The goal of accuracy also requires that the process of generalization itself must be subject to scrutiny. Therefore, the anthropologist should indicate what his evidence consists of (his observations, interviews, or the like); how he analyzed, classified, or sorted this evidence into more general categories; how these categories themselves were compared or contrasted; and finally, how his conclusions follow logically from the evidence.

It is unfortunate that ethnographic reports do not always provide enough information of these kinds for the reader to confidently judge their accuracy. Until recently, anthropologists often neglected these questions; and nonanthropologists who have done ethnographic writing typically still do. As a result, our efforts to judge an account's accuracy must sometimes be intuitive. In such instances, we ask whether an ethnographic report "makes sense." Is it credible, given what we know of other people in other societies? This question of credibility arises most acutely when the writer has not been trained in anthropology and when his motives for writing are not known to include a search for truth. The accuracy of travelers' tales, for example, has always been suspect to the anthropologist. Indeed, often such reports contain nothing of ethnographic value; an example is André Gide's *Travels in the Congo* (1929). Or they are so obviously fabricated that they cannot be taken seriously, as Captain J. A. Lawson's *Travels in New Guinea* (1875). On the other hand, tales that are true are sometimes not believed, as British explorer James Bruce discovered upon returning from his remarkable journey to the Nile in 1769 and 1770.

> . . . The secretary Luigi Balugani died at Gondar, and so Bruce is the only eye-witness of what befell the two men there; his account cannot be checked by either collaborators or contemporaries. Like Marco Polo he tells an intensely personal story, and the people he writes about so confidently were then as strange to Europe and the civilized world as the denizens of outer space are to us today. On his return, says his biographer, Francis Head, he told the public of people who wore rings in their lips instead of their ears—who anointed themselves not with bear's grease or pomatum, but with the blood of cows—who, instead of playing tunes upon them, wore the entrails of animals as ornaments—and who, instead of eating hot putrid meat, licked their lips over bleeding living flesh. He described debauchery dreadfully disgusting, because it was so different to their own. He told of men who hunted each other—of mothers who had not seen ten winters—and he described crowds of human beings and huge animals retreating in terror before an army of little flies! In short, he told them the truth, and nothing but the truth; but . . . the facts he related were too strong. (Moorehead, 1962:18-19)

It is not only travelers of the eighteenth and nineteenth centuries whose "ethnographic" reports can meet with disbelief. Colin Turnbull is a British-trained anthropologist whose fieldwork with the BaMbuti Pygmies of the Ituri Forest is reported in books that have been generally acclaimed for their literary as well as scientific value. In 1972 he published *The Mountain People*, an account of life among the Ik of Uganda. Largely because of drought, the Ik were quite literally starving. Turnbull reported their lives and their deaths in detail. He also reported their progressive isolation from each other as they sought to find food and to live a little longer. He said that they had lost the last vestiges of human love for each other and with it had lost their humanity. What is more, he suggested that signs of the same individualization seen among the Ik could be seen developing in the West. What Turnbull described was shocking: mothers unmoved by the death of their children, children competing desperately for a morsel of food, the strong prying

A Central African's Description of a European Woman.—
Magaga, one of the Wanyamwezi, saw an English lady at Zanzibar,
and describes her thus: "I saw a white woman at Zanzibar; she
had fastened a lot of cloth about her belly like a *Mrua* [a race of
the Upper Congo], but she wore most of the pieces of cloth
bundled together behind her, while the *Mrua* wears it in front.   She
had hidden her feet and hands in black and yellow bags, just as she
overwhelmed her whole body with cloth.   Her body was the ugliest
thing about her—as thin round the belly as an insect ; so that you
would have been able to break it without much straining of your
strength.   She had tied her breast up high, so that she looked like
a young maiden.   But that was only a lie ; she was an old woman—
quite old ; in spite of her lie, I saw that.   Her face was very white.
On her head she had a *Ngalla* (warrior's head-dress) of ostrich
feathers, very high, of beautiful feathers.   (This seemed to interest
Maganga the most.   He shook with laughter).   She wore ear-rings
like our women, and her step was like a man's.   *I-icsch ! Wasunga !*
But I wouldn't like to have such an ugly wife, with a waist like an
insect."—(Paul Reichard, "Die Wanjamwesi," *Zeitsch. Gesell. f.
Erdkundi*, Berlin, vol. 24, pt. 4, 1889, p. 253.)

JOHN MURDOCH.

CULTURAL BIAS? Ethnocentric assumptions are not limited to anthropologists. (A note from
American Anthropologist, 4:328, October, 1891)

open the jaws of the weak to take their food, and everyone laughing at the misery of
others. Turnbull's book, like Bruce's, is too strong for some. His interpretations
have been criticized by anthropologists and the general public alike, who argue
that his conclusions do not necessarily follow from his evidence. Others have
questioned the evidence itself, asking whether Turnbull—who admits that he
regards love as the highest human value—was biased and did not therefore observe
and report the Ik in an unduly negative light. How can we judge? Turnbull does not
give us the details we need to judge his accuracy, so we must use intuition in
assessing Turnbull's evidence and his efforts to be objective. We read his earlier
books for clues to his skill as a fieldworker. We compare his account of the Ik with
what we know of other peoples in similar circumstances. If we are unsatisfied, we
look for independent sources of information. In this instance, unfortunately,
almost nothing is known about the Ik beyond what Turnbull has written.

Peter Matthiessen's ethnographic book *Under the Mountain Wall* (1962) met a different reception. Matthiessen, a naturalist and writer, accompanied the Harvard-Peabody Expedition of 1961 which spent its time in the remote Baliem Valley of West Irian (Irian Barat). The book, which is "a chronicle of two seasons in the Stone Age," is a remarkable account of warfare, revenge, death, mourning, and to a lesser extent, life in general. The book was "inspected" by Karl Heider and Jan Broekhuyse, both anthropologists, who agreed that "within the limits of our present understanding of the culture it attempts an honest portrait of the Kurelu" (Matthiessen, 1962:xiv). There is no reason to suppose it is not a perfectly true account. This is not to say there was no selectivity or distortion at all, and there are, perhaps, brief lapses into poetic license; but books by anthropologists can have the same shortcomings.

Correspondingly high quality has characterized books written by wives of anthropologists, in part perhaps because they had professionals (their husbands) available for consultation about ethnographic details and presentations. Moreover, many of these wives have been closely involved in the collection of the field data; others have simply been especially sensitive observers of the social scene. For whatever combination of reasons, they have produced some remarkably fine books. *The Fon of Bafut* (Ritzenthaler, 1966), *The House of Lim* (Margery Wolf, 1968), and *Guests of the Sheik* (Fernea, 1965) are the best examples. Thus far, husbands of female anthropologists have not written similar books, but there is a growing trend for men to go into the field with their anthropologist wives, so a parallel may soon develop.

Not all laymen who attempt to write true ethnographic accounts are fortunate enough to have one or more anthropologists along as consultants. Does that mean their descriptions and interpretations are any the less true? It may indeed, as it is entirely possible that an untrained observer would misinterpret some particular custom, whereas an anthropologist, more familiar with a range of customs and practices, is less likely to misunderstand. But in so far as an author describes faithfully what he saw and heard, lack of anthropological training need not be a problem. Consider Farley Mowat's *People of the Deer* (1952). Mowat lived during an extended period with the Eskimo of the Great Barrens, learned their language, and gave us lengthy descriptions of their culture. His book is readable and entertaining, and there is no reason to assume it contains any serious distortions of fact. One might well contrast such a book with Tobias Schneebaum's *Keep the River on Your Right* (1969), which offers very little in the way of ethnographic detail and is far too introspective to be useful as an account of other people and their culture.

Consider also the well-known book *Kabloona* by Gontran de Poncins. Poncins's goal, as he describes it, is no different from the usual goal of the anthropologist, and he is probably equally successful in achieving it.

From all that I have said, it will I hope be clear that there is no fiction in this book. Here and there I have made assumptions concerning what was going on in the mind of one or another of the Eskimos with whom I lived. It is possible that an assumption here or there is inaccurate: if so, the inaccuracy is the product of ignorance and not of intent. As for the physical and material life of the Eskimo, I have set that down as I saw it with my own eyes. I do not insist that other travellers may not have seen other Eskimos proceed differently. (1941:ix)

Should we accept travelers' accounts as accurate in the same way we accept the accounts of anthropologists? In fact, we often do. The only information we have on certain cultures has come from travelers' accounts, or from the accounts of missionaries, traders, and other nonanthropologists. Several fine ethnographic descriptions of other cultures are accepted widely by anthropologists although written by laymen. For example, Knud Rasmussen and Peter Freuchen both produced accurate and detailed ethnographic records on the Eskimo although by today's standards neither was an anthropologist. During the last century it was impossible, in many cases, to distinguish between anthropology and travel. Everard F. ImThurn's *Among the Indians of Guiana* (1883), was accepted as not only a record of his travels but also a definitive treatise on the ethnography, botany, and zoology of the area. J. G. Kohl's *Kitchi-Gami: Wanderings Round Lake Superior* (1860) has long been regarded as an exceptional ethnographic document. And the influence of such books as *The Travels of Marco Polo* and *Travels in Arabia Deserta* has been simply incalculable. Mention must also be made here of the remarkable personal account of Daisy Bates, who lived with Australian aborigines for thirty-five years. Her *The Passing of the Aborigines* (1938) is a fascinating book, containing much accurate ethnographic information as well as an account of her own work and attitudes.

In many books, usually by explorers or travelers, the ethnographic details are made so subservient to the prose style and experiences of the author that they become mere sidelights or passing comments instead of the author's major interest. *People of the Reeds* (Maxwell, 1957) and *The Marsh Arabs* (Thesiger, 1964) tend to be books of this type.

It is clear from an examination of books such as these that anthropologists have no unique claim to ethnographic accuracy; but it is also apparent that readers of works by nonanthropologists must digest carefully what they are told, consider the motives and methods of the authors, and reflect seriously about the evidence presented before accepting uncritically what they are reading. In general, books written by laymen are far more likely to contain errors of fact or interpretation than books by anthropologists.

In ethnographic writing, as in any other scientific presentation, the goal of accuracy goes hand in hand with the goal of efficiency. This goal is seen in the general understanding among scientists that if two accounts contain the same amount of accurate information, then the shorter account is the better one. Efficiency is valued because anthropologists are overwhelmed with written material and want to extract from it as much information as possible in the shortest amount of time. For the ethnographic writer, however, there is the additional constraint of space. The longest book he can hope to have published would rarely run over 500 pages or so; most ethnographic accounts are shorter than this. The goal of efficiency calls for a concise writing style that leaves no room for literary flourishes or personal reminiscences. It also calls for technical language that can convey a complex meaning in a single term. Thus, anthropologists, like other scientists, use technical terms such as "acculturation," "affinal kinship," "agnatic descent," "cross-cousin marriage," "exogamy," "prescriptive alliance" and the like, and they give very precise definitions to such common terms as "family," "law," "joking," "marriage," "myth," "status," "religion," and "warfare." The result is a technical language that seems to be a jargon to the outsider. Technical language can be abused or overused, and then it deserves the epithet "jargon," but it can also be an essential means of efficient communication. The overuse of jargon and the failure to write clearly and simply drove the eminent literary critic Edmund Wilson to this famous comment:

> As for my experience with articles by experts in anthropology and sociology, it has led me to conclude that the requirement in my ideal university, of having the papers in every department passed by a professor of English, might result in revolutionizing these subjects—if indeed the second of them survived at all. (1956:164)

The audience one writes for is an important consideration. Some anthropologists write ethnographic books for the general reading public (and we shall discuss this kind of writing later on), but most write primarily for an audience of fellow anthropologists. For this audience the goals are accuracy and efficiency. The writing itself should be clear, simple, and precise (although often it is none of these).

Anthropologists typically publish their fieldwork data for use by an audience of other anthropologists, either in a journal article or in an ethnographic monograph. (Anthropologists also write works of theoretical interest, which we will discuss in Part III of this book.)

In the journal article, space is limited and so is the range of subject matter, which is usually a specialized treatment of data with some importance for method or theory. Conciseness and efficiency must be the goals when most articles seldom exceed twenty pages. These articles are an important means of scientific communication in anthropology, but the results of fieldwork—the ethnographic description of the culture of a particular people—cannot be confined to the space of an article. Thus anthropologists have made extensive use of the longer monograph—the scholarly account of the culture of a particular people—as the primary medium for their ethnographic writing.

There is no "standard" monograph, any more than there is an average man, but we can speak of the typical monograph, characterized by certain distinctive features. First, it has no plot. There is no story, or even chronology of events. Second, there are no characters. Indeed, individuals appear only in anecdotal illustrations, or are sometimes recognized for their help as informants in the acknowledgments.

The ethnographer's account does not evoke for his readers a sense of life in the society as he actually witnessed it, because the anthropologist is writing about an abstract and generalized cultural pattern derived from these real-life events. Acts and persons in the monograph are taken from the natural context in which they originally occurred. Personality and other idiosyncratic elements of the scene drop out. Social behaviors are separated off and classed into various "roles"; individuals disappear into "statuses," "groups," and "classes" of various types. Sets of events which in real life were separated widely in time are placed side by side in the description in order to emphasize their linkages. The only portions of ethnographies that typically retain naturalistic accounts of events the anthropologist witnessed are anecdotes and short episodes that serve to provide a sample of the data on which generalizations have been based.

The cultural pattern that the anthropologist describes is made up of interrelated parts. This fact accounts for his original holistic approach in gathering his field data. It also makes his task of reporting more difficult, as he must try to decide how best to divide the cultural whole in order to discuss it. Anthropologists usually present their material under subject headings that traditionally include: location and environment, technology and economics, kinship and social organization, law and social control, politics, religion, and the arts. They may sometimes include a chapter on history, but often this is impossible to reconstruct. Otherwise the presentation is static in time except for some discussion of an average day, the typical life cycle of a person, or the annual cycle of activities. There may also be appendices that contain specialized data. The goal of holism, in which all parts of the culture are presented in their relationships to each other, is an ideal but one that is seldom achieved as well as the writer would like.

An example of an ethnographic monograph that follows this standard format is Clyde Kluckhohn and Dorothea Leighton's well-known study, *The Navaho*, originally published in 1946 and reprinted in 1962. The monograph has major sections called "The Past of the People" (their earliest history to the present day), "Land and Livelihood" (all aspects of technology and economy), "Living Together" (everything from physical appearance, everyday life in the family, to the wider circles of kinship, leadership, and authority), "The People and the World Around Them" (their relations with other Indians, whites, and their government, both tribal and federal), "The Supernatural: Power and Danger" (beings and powers, ghosts, witches, theories of disease, folk tales, and myths), "The Supernatural: Things to Do and Not to Do" (values, attitudes, sanctions, birth, initiation, ceremonies, curing, other rites and the like), "The Meaning of the Supernatural" (economic and social aspects of ceremonials, what myths and rites do for the individual and the group, the gain and cost of witchcraft), "The Tongue of the People" (Navaho sounds, words, grammar, and the social meaning of language),

"The Navaho View of Life" (ethics, values, premises of life and thought, world view). All this is presented in a little over 300 pages.

This sort of all-purpose ethnographic monograph is less common today. For one thing, some anthropologists believe there are already enough general monographs to provide a record of the cultures of most peoples of the world. But many anthropologists also believe, and no doubt rightly, that no culture can be adequately described in a single monograph. They therefore prefer more specialized monographs on kinship, religion, economics, social organization, or the like, although the emphasis often remains holistic with the subject seen in context and in relation to other aspects of culture. Some anthropologists have written several specialized monographs about a single people. As was mentioned earlier, Franz Boas wrote over 5000 pages about the Kwakiutl; Malinowski wrote four monographs about the Trobriand Islanders; and Evans-Pritchard has written several monographs about the Nuer.

Whether ethnographic monographs deal with all of a culture or only part of it, they are usually dull and difficult to read—perhaps inevitably since the goal of a monograph is to convey a generalized account of various patterns of culture to other professional anthropologists. For example, the Crow Indians of the Northern Plains are the subject of a famous monograph by Robert Lowie (1935). The monograph covers many aspects of Crow culture and is based upon Lowie's several field trips to the Crow. The book is intelligent and in places there are flashes of insight and humor. Yet it cannot compare for insight, humor, drama, and pathos with the story of the Crow chief Plenty-coups, as told to Frank Linderman (1930). Lowie's job was a generalized description of Crow culture—almost in its entirety; Plenty-coups was telling about the most meaningful and dramatic aspects of his life. The differences are obvious.

To illustrate these differences, let us compare two books by the same anthropologist, Colin Turnbull. His book *The Forest People* (1961) is a personalized account of Turnbull's fieldwork experiences with the Pygmies of the Ituri forest. In it Turnbull presents a fascinating, exciting, poignant story of the life of these people. Individual Pygmies become the actors in the drama and their lives and problems are highlighted. Thanks to Turnbull's skill, the lives of these various individuals lead us to an understanding of the culture itself. So skillful is Turnbull's writing that these people come alive for the reader who can understand their cultural differences yet empathize with their humanity. The book is of value to anthropologists and has been widely read and used by them, but it has also been read and enjoyed by the general public. After writing *The Forest People*, and despite its professional and public success, Turnbull wrote an ethnographic monograph about the same culture. This monograph, *Wayward Servants* (1965), covers all aspects of Pygmy culture in technical detail. It is a solid professional achievement, of clear value to anthropologists. Yet despite Turnbull's gifts as a writer, this book has no appeal to the general public. It is, relatively speaking, dull and technical. Witness the following statement about the potentially lively subject of marriage:

Betrothal and marriage among the Mbuti, then, are permissive. Prescriptions and prohibitions are minimal, and even preferences are not dominant. But permission of the band or bands involved is required. In giving assent a band does not concern itself with the niceties of the kinship relationships involved, nor with the question of reciprocal obligations and privileges, except for the question of sister exchange. While not expecting an immediate exchange to be made, or even asking for a suitable future exchange partner to be named, the band bears this reciprocal obligation in mind and will demand that it be fulfilled the moment such fulfillment becomes necessary to band composition. (1965:141)

Many passages in this monograph are every bit as generalized as this one, and far more technical. Nothing of this generalized, analytic sort appears in *The Forest People*. *The Forest People* gives us a memorable glimpse into the world of the Mbuti as they live in it and understand it. Through its presentation of actual people and specific events *The Forest People* permits us to grasp something of the motivations, thoughts, and emotions of these people. But the book does not tell us all that we wish to know about the patterns of their behavior or about the rules that lie behind these patterns. For this information, we must turn to *Wayward Servants*. The difference lies in the goals of the books.

Ethnographic monographs, more than any other source, provide us with our understanding of other cultures, and thus teach us about human differences and similarities over the face of the earth. As we shall see in Part III, the search for general principles of human behavior in various societies is based almost exclusively on monographs of this kind. These monographs are extremely valuable in providing accurate, generalized summaries of culture; our knowledge of human behavior would be much poorer without them. Yet the truth they convey is a special kind. It is generalized and therefore omits much of a culture's variation and deviance, complexity and ambiguity. It is abstract and concerned with cultural patterns, so it omits much about individuals and their emotions, their motives, their joys, and their hopes. It is short and efficient, so it cannot develop a sense of drama, of life as it is lived every day in the emotion-charged, complex, changing, contradictory way we have come to expect from real life. In the search for general patterns, the standard monograph achieves one truth but loses another—the particular and human realities of individual persons and events. Because some anthropologists want to go beyond the generalized accounts of ethnographic monographs toward other dimensions of truth about humans and their culture, and because they want to present their accounts to a more general audience, other styles of presenting ethnographic data have been developed.

Other Styles: Humanistic Ethnography

C. P. Snow's famous works have dramatized the differences between science and humanism. As Snow correctly points out, humanism as epitomized by literature and art has come to be seen as something that differs fundamentally from science (1959). These differences are considered to include basic goals, procedures, and products. Despite a long tradition of humanism in anthropology, science has long dominated anthropology's styles of presentation, so much so, in fact, that anthropologists who departed from the scientific style of ethnographic writing have often come in for criticism. They have been accused of courting the general public for adulation or profit, of abandoning science for literature, or of becoming "mere" journalists. Such criticisms are perhaps less common than they once were, but the attitude comprised in Snow's view of two competing and irreconcilable ways of knowing—the scientific and the humanistic—has continued to affect the ways anthropologists present their ethnographic information.

Is humanism basically different from science? It can be. Humanism may differ from science by failing to make accuracy its primary goal; thus humanistic writing may be highly symbolic, metaphorical, or personal. Humanistic writing may be designed to entertain, and its methods may be that of dramatic exaggeration or subtle irony. It may also seek not to describe or understand an existing reality, but to construct a new or more beautiful one. But is a humanistic presentation *necessarily* different from a scientific one? Several basic distinctions between the two have been suggested.

It has been suggested that scientific ethnography is set off from literary forms of reporting by its objectivity. Literature is said to be subjective or sentimental:

Sentimentality is the enemy of anthropology. To write with understanding of people whose institutions and beliefs are alien requires the anthropologist to make an effort to see them as they are and to portray them as he sees them. He must view them in the round and strive to penetrate the meaning of their behavior through the language they use. (Freedman, 1968:xii)

However, non-scientific literature, even fiction, also contains many examples of objective writing. Compare the comment above with this discussion of the nineteenth-century French novelist Gustave Flaubert:

Having no model to look to, except possibly Balzac, whose hortatory style he found distasteful, Flaubert was obliged to invent his own style. This has been variously described as "writing with a scalpel" and as "objective seriousness." One of its essentials is its disciplined objectivity: Flaubert never tells you what you ought to think of the events he sets before you, nor even what he himself thinks. . . . Flaubert sets down reality as precisely as he can, and that is as much as we get from him. (Tomkievicz, 1971:115)

The tradition of realism, which has had a long history in literature, has goals which sound remarkably like those claimed for ethnography: ". . . the realist . . . is interested in telling the truth, as he sees it, about the world he has come in contact with" (Maugham, 1969:46). The earliest definition of the novel, and one which is often employed today with only slight modifications, portrays the novel in a way which makes it sound no different from a standard, "scientific" ethnography: "The Novel is a picture of real life and manners, and of the time in which it is written" (Reeve, 1785). Tolstoy is regarded by some as having given "a complete picture of the Russia of that day" (Strakhov, quoted in Maugham, 1969:258); and Balzac set out to, and did—more or less—chronicle "the history of manners and customs" of his time:

> In 1833 he conceived the idea of combining the whole of his production into one whole under the name of *La Comédie Humaine*. When it occurred to him, he ran to see his sister: "Salute me," he cried, "because I'm quite plainly (*tout simplement*) on the way to become a genius." He described as follows what he had in mind: "The social world of France would be the historian, I should be merely the secretary. In setting forth an inventory of vices and virtues, in assembling the principal facts of the passions, in painting characters, in choosing the principal incidents of the social world, in composing types by combining the traits of several homogeneous characters, perhaps I could manage to write the history forgotten by so many historians, the history of manners and customs." (Maugham, 1969:120)

The concept of culture was introduced into the English language much later than 1833; "manners and customs" is a close substitute.

We have seen that other literature can share the subject matter as well as the objective attitude of the more standard ethnographic presentation. Methods of data collection do not serve to distinguish the two, either. There have been many instances of nonanthropologist writers using methods that were essentially anthropological to gather their material. Many writers, wishing to depict some aspect of life in another culture, spend substantial periods soaking up "background." The procedures used are often like those of participant-observation. Farley Mowat lived for two years with the Eskimo of the Great Barrens and came to speak their language well before writing *People of the Deer* (1952). Truman Capote is said to have developed observational, interviewing, and recording techniques identical to those employed by anthropologists; these made possible his essentially ethnographic study of the American midwest, *In Cold Blood* (1965).

It has also been said that ethnographies are somehow more "scientific" than other forms of writing because they deal with abstractions and make generalizations rather than depicting the specific details of a particular event. It seems more reasonable to see the particular and the general not as opposing tendencies, but as parts of a single process. Kaplan, a philosopher of science, makes the point that any generalization must be based upon solid "particular" facts:

> . . . The emphasis on the importance to behavioral science of coming to understand real particulars is, I believe, a healthy one, for often the scholar preoccupied with historical movements, forces, and institutions rather than with the lives of men is more likely to be writing fiction than the novelist. But for science, what is rooted in the particularity of fact comes to flower in the generalization of theory—or else it fails to seed. (Kaplan, 1964:118-119)

The value of the particular case for illustrating and affirming a generalization or abstraction has long been recognized by all anthropologists. This technique is a part of the repertoire of ethnographic writers, used to convey a sense of the original data on which their generalizations are based. There have also been deliberate attempts to weld the specific with the general, as in Victor Turner's use of "social dramas" (1957).

The anthropologist Hortense Powdermaker, with her long anthropological experience, has provided this perspective:

> The novelist and playwright, as well as the anthropologist, write out of their immersion and participation in a particular situation from which they have been able to detach themselves. But they write of the particular; if they are gifted, the particular illuminates the human condition. The anthropologist starts with particulars, and then analyzes, generalizes, and compares; the gifted ones may also illuminate the human condition. (1966:296)

The scientific tradition in anthropology has led to a distinction between humanistic writers, who are said to be creative, and anthropologists, who are asserted to be scientific instruments, recorders. Thus the anthropologist Eric Wolf has written:

> . . .The writer . . . creates his work of art; the anthropologist, to the contrary, describes and analyzes a phenomenon he has done nothing to create. The work of art with which the anthropologist is concerned exists when he comes to it—it is the culture wrought by Siuai or Tikopia or the people of Atimelang—all he can do is capture the phenomenon with fidelity and insight. (1964:90)

It is true that anthropologists do not create the cultures they write about, but as they try to "capture" these cultures on paper with "fidelity," they do generalize and thereby produce a new reality. If their work is accurate, this new reality is only a condensed version of the larger reality from which it was taken. But anthropologists may also see cultures in ways that members of these cultures do not. When Ruth Benedict depicted the Zuñi as Apollonian, the Zuñi were not asked to affirm this truth. What is more, it was not a depiction—true or not—which they could have affirmed. It was a new reality, created by Benedict. Hence, while it is true that anthropologists are primarily concerned with accuracy and thus try above all to be true to the phenomena of the culture they study, nevertheless all writers create by the very act of writing a reality that has never existed before.

While other forms of literature are free to vary from the standards that have been set for writing ethnographies—and generally do—the same scientific goals and methods that are associated with writing ethnographies can accompany these other literary styles as well. Insistence on a clear distinction between ethnography and literature or between science and the humanities is misleading. Each effort to depict life in another culture, whether it be done in standard ethnographic form or other, must be judged on its own merits for what it sets out to accomplish, how well it succeeds in its goal, and how accurately it presents some aspect of culture. The question of whether anthropology should be scientific or humanistic should cease to disturb us once we understand the richness and the dual nature of anthropology:

If the dual nature of anthropology—an art and a science, a humanistic science—is accepted, there is no reason why each cannot be expanded. The inherent ambiguities of this approach are only a reflection of those which exist in life itself. (Powdermaker, 1966:206)

In what follows we will attempt to expand on and clarify the more humanistic aspects of anthropology as these are seen in efforts to present truths about human behavior that standard ethnographies seldom include.

The Ethnographic Novel

The tradition of humanistic anthropology in America can be traced back at least as far as 1890. In that year Adolph Bandelier published his novel of the Keresan Pueblos called *The Delight Makers*. Bandelier, like many of the early scholars, was an archaeologist, historian, and ethnographer all in one. His reasons for writing his materials in the form of a novel are interesting:

> . . . I was prompted to perform the work by a conviction that however scientific works may tell the truth about the Indian they exercise always a limited influence upon the general public; and to that public, in our country as well as abroad, the Indian has remained as good as unknown. By clothing sober facts in the garb of romance I have hoped to make the "Truth about the Pueblo Indians" more accessible and perhaps more acceptable to the public in general. (1890: Preface)

The "sober facts" Bandelier desired to convey, he went on, were "divided into three classes—geographical, ethnological, and archaeological." But basically the book was a novel of suspense, intrigue, and human foibles. It was based in some measure on Bandelier's imagination, taking place at a time in the past, but it also drew importantly from ethnographic observations he had actually made, and succeeded in conveying a great deal about Pueblo life.

As it is clear that Bandelier's primary aim in writing *The Delight Makers* was to convey ethnographic facts to the public, we might say the book is the first of a number of what we will term ethnographic novels. *The Delight Makers* managed to convey a great deal of accurate, useful, ethnographic information. It was marred, however, by a certain amount of ethnocentrism which, in 1890, was not uncommon even in anthropology.

Bandelier wrote, ". . .for the Indian speaks like a child, using figures of speech, not in order to embellish, but because he lacks abstract terms and is compelled to borrow equivalents from comparisons with surrounding nature" (1890:165). And again, ". . .He is a child, and children rarely make atonement unless compelled" (1890:303). Comparing children with "primitive" people was quite common at this time and, although ethnocentrism is still a problem at times in anthropology, it is rarely as blatant now as it was in this early period. Despite this flaw, Bandelier's book was not only accepted by the general reading public but was highly regarded by anthropologists as well, as we see in the remarks that A. L. Kroeber made thirty-odd years later, ". . . this novel still renders a more comprehensive and coherent view of native Pueblo life than any scientific volume on the Southwest" (1922:13). It was the first of a new but still very limited genre, which includes *Eskimo* (Freuchen, 1931), *Flesh of the Wild Ox: A Riffian Chronicle of High Valleys and Long Rifles* (Coon, 1932), *The Golden Wing* (Lin Yueh-hwa, 1947), *Tents against the Sky* (Ekvall, 1954), and *Bite of Hunger* (Kuper, 1965), among others.

Ethnographic novels might be distinguished from other kinds of novels by their attempt to cross a cultural boundary. Most novelists write for and about members of the same culture, hence have no problems with "translating" cultural acts and feelings across a cultural boundary. Writing about another people in an "exotic" or remote culture is more difficult. Bandelier speaks at one point in his book of "horrid masks." But are these masks "horrid" to the Indians or "horrid" in the eyes of Bandelier? Unless the novelist keeps a clear distinction between reporting the inner view of the culture he is writing about and reporting the view of an outsider, his work becomes open to ambiguity in the interpretation of the ethnographic facts he presents. Furthermore, if his goal is to convey the actual feelings and thoughts of the members of another culture—as Bandelier's goal was—then he must do so in a way which leads the reader to a comprehension of how and why these persons feel and act as they do. Without this appreciation, there can be no empathy or understanding, and the motives and actions of persons in other cultures seem inexplicable, perhaps shocking, or even disgusting.

Another problem that the ethnographer-novelist faces involves the often contradictory goals of telling a good story and explaining the ethnographic facts of another culture. When the writer explains more than the reader needs to know to understand the story, such explanation becomes intrusive; the characters no longer seem real but are merely the creations of a didactic author, and the writer loses rapport with resentful readers, rapport which is necessary if readers are to understand his characters and the culture in which they live. The dangers of overzealous presentation of ethnographic detail can be seen in the following quotation from a review of James Houston's *The White Dawn* (1971):

> I should say at once that I enjoyed this story, or essay on Eskimo cultural anthropology, or whatever it is, but I did not enjoy it as a novel. . . . Houston slips an extraordinary quantity of anthropological information into his story: how igloos are built and a bed made of skins, how polar bears are killed and a shaman works his magic. But, as I say, about the time of the walrus hunt I realized that the information was the point of the book. The novel's didacticism finally becomes intrusive—to the point where the story, finally, counts for little. (Prescott, 1971:65)

In the same way that ethnographic fiction can falter by being forced to accommodate too much ethnographic fact, it can suffer from too much sociologizing. Consider Lin Yueh-hwa's *The Golden Wing* (1947). This is, according to

Raymond Firth's introduction, "a sociological study written in the form of a novel" (1947:xi). It is an ethnographic novel as well, and it is fascinating to observe the author's use of ethnographic descriptions and sociological generalizations. At times he takes a direct approach which may be jarring to the reader's sense of involvement in the story: "A little explanation may be needed about the native banks. These banks did not necessarily have much capital" (1947:8). At other times, however, he weaves ethnographic fact neatly into the story: "To help cut the family expenses, Aunt Lin availed herself of an old local custom and gave her youngest child to another family, as a betrothed daughter to be adopted into the other family's households" (1947:16). Sometimes he seems to review his field notes: "All the neighbours and relatives who came to hear the glad news were offered eggs and noodles. The noodles signified long life and the eggs, peace. The eggs were dyed red, for that is the colour that represents happiness" (1947:20).

Lin Yueh-hwa may also insert his sociology lessons into the minds of his characters: "He considered attending an act of filial piety. Likewise, he knew that the reunion of the clan, in which all their personal ties were renewed, was one of the great integrating forces of the village" (1947:63).

The Golden Wing is an important and valuable ethnographic document, but it suffers as an artistic production. There is great literary skill and ingenuity involved in successfully weaving ethnographic data into a narrative account. A Western audience is not accustomed to finding statements such as the following inserted into their novels:

> This gathering served as a means by which the social ties between people could be renewed. Performance of the ceremonies fulfilled both the duty of the living to the dead and the obligations of all the people associated with them to the afflicted family. Tradition thus carried on from one generation to the next gives scope for a renewal of the integration of the social group. (1947:110)

If a writer is unable to find a more graceful and appropriate way to incorporate such information into his novel, then he must expect to lose a portion of the benefits he had hoped to gain by choosing the novelistic form in the first place.

Judged from another perspective, that of scientific merit, Lin Yueh-hwa's novel might be accorded high marks for attempting to give a thorough portrait of the culture and sociology of a Chinese village. Ethnographic novels, if they omit large amounts of information and are too selective, can leave the reader with a distorted picture of life in another society. This is a common fault of the ethnographic novels written by nonanthropologists. Such writers are more concerned with spinning an entertaining story than they are with giving their readers an accurate insight into another culture. It is a well-known fact that the different and more sensational features of another way of life will catch the reader's interest while the more mundane may simply bore him.

Ethnographic novels can be placed on a continuum from those, usually written by anthropologists, designed primarily to acquaint the reader with life in another culture to those, usually written by nonanthropologists, that use ethnographic fact and description as exotic background for their story. *Deep Valley* (1971), by a pair of anthropologists, the Aginskys, is an example of the first type of writing; Peter Matthiessen's *At Play in the Fields of the Lord* (1965) is an example of the latter. It is important, therefore, that the reader take into consideration both the credentials and the goals of a writer when judging how likely it is that a particular ethnographic novel presents an accurate account of the life of people in a different culture.

Humanistic anthropology, in recent years, has by no means been encouraged to the same extent as scientific anthropology. Thus many of its practitioners have written under pseudonyms or have prefaced their works with apologies. The following is a good example:

> It is with some amount of reluctance that we present this volume to the public because it is an innovation we fear may be misunderstood and thought to be a fictional account rather than the result of twenty-five years of library and field research. However, we feel that the value of showing an American aboriginal culture in a form in which the people act and speak as they did previous to white contact warrants the attempt. (Aginsky and Aginsky, 1971:7)

As we have seen, there are difficulties with the ethnographic novel that can reduce its effectiveness as literature or as ethnography. But when the novel is constructed to reveal the inner life of people—their values, feelings, and ways of thinking—it can be a valuable device for presenting the insider's view in context. Such novels can be entertaining and can add a dimension to our ethnographic understanding. There need be no apologies.

Ethnographic Short Stories, Tales, Anecdotes

When myths, short stories, and anecdotes from another culture are translated with fidelity, they usually are neither understood nor appreciated by a Western audience. For instance, one anthropologist experimented with reading American Indian tales to his children at bedtime. They found the structure and the story line incomprehensible and soon rejected the tales for a more familiar type of story.

While it is true that tales from a literary tradition which differs only slightly from one's own may not only be accepted but may even become classics—witness the popularity of *The Arabian Nights*—it is also true that most literary productions from another society demand a background of cultural explanation before they can be appreciated at all. Attempts to present this kind of material to a general audience are rare. It is much more usual for writers to operate within their own literary traditions when presenting tales of another way of life.

It has been fairly common for travelers, missionaries, and traders to write brief accounts of their experiences. Some of these are in the form of short stories, some are merely tales that were heard and recorded, and some are anecdotes. Both Knud

Rasmussen and Peter Freuchen, who gave us vast amounts of ethnographic information about the Eskimo at an early date, wrote in this vein. Rasmussen's *The People of the Polar North* (1908) is a collection of this type, as is Freuchen's *Book of the Eskimo* (1961).

Anthropologists have also attempted to write ethnographic short stories and tales. In 1922, a collection of such writings appeared, entitled *American Indian Life*. The roster of authors included names of some of the most famous anthropologists of the time: Robert Lowie, Clark Wissler, Paul Radin, Frank G. Speck, Leslie Spier, Alfred M. Tozzer, Edward Sapir, A. L. Kroeber, and Franz Boas himself. In the introduction by A. L. Kroeber, the point was made that it is important for anthropologists to write for the general reader. The method of the short story was lauded for allowing the anthropologists to present "psychological aspects of Indian culture" (Parsons, 1922:2) which they would otherwise not attempt:

> . . .This psychology of the Indian is often expressed by the frontiersman, the missionary and trader, by the man of the city, even. But it has been very little formulated by the very men who know most, who have each given a large block of their lives to acquiring intensive and exact information about the Indian and his culture. (Kroeber, 1922:13)

The fictional nature of the short stories was not regarded as a handicap. Indeed, the authors felt that it had positive merit. Kroeber's statement of what they were attempting is most enlightening on this point:

> The fictional form of presentation devised by the editor has definite merit. It allows a freedom in depicting or suggesting the thoughts and feelings of the Indian, such as is impossible in a formal, scientific report. In fact, it incites to active psychological treatment, else the tale would lag. At the same time the customs depicted are never invented. Each author has adhered strictly to the social facts as he knew them. He has merely selected those that seemed most characteristic and woven them into a plot around an imaginary Indian hero or heroine. The method is that of the historical novel, with the emphasis on the history rather than the romance. (1922:13)

There are several things of interest about this attempt. First, it was an early attempt by anthropologists to say something about individual psychology as well as culture. Second, there is no suggestion that it is in any way undesirable, improper, or unprofessional for anthropologists to attempt to write in this prose style; the book was written before it had become so important to anthropologists to be identified as scientists. Third, the anthropologists seem to feel no doubt either that they could understand the psychology of Indians or could write about it in a prose style with which they were unfamiliar and for which they were untrained. While their output did satisfy the needs of ethnography, perhaps, it resulted in rather poor prose. The book was not particularly well received. Nonetheless, it was an early example of humanistic anthropology. Had the approach been pursued further, perhaps anthropologists could have learned to write prose, at least better than they characteristically do. But humanistic anthropology, as a tradition, tended to go underground after this—not because of the poor prose, but because anthropology felt it had to become scientific.

Although many anthropologists, today and in the past, have received psychological training, the question of *communicating* psychological facts cross-culturally has rarely been considered. In how many contexts could one use the notion of romantic love, for example? Do the characters in the pieces attribute motives to each other at all? Do they experience jealousy? Guilt? Do they understand profit and loss? All our experiences indicate that men everywhere share the same types of emotions; the differences lie in the situations that call these emotions forth and the way in which they are expressed. How does one draw characters and depict their actions and motives convincingly for an audience of outsiders? Can one remain faithful to the psychological realities of another culture and still keep one's reading audience? These questions must be pondered well when considering attempts to translate the psychological reality of one culture into the literary requirements for psychological reality in another.

American Indian Life was not a completely isolated event in American anthropology. Other anthropologists at this time also wrote fictional or semifictional short stories and tales. But no formal tradition of such anthropology emerged. Nor was much thought given to writing styles, the problems of cross-cultural communication, the audience, or the purposes to which the materials might be put. It was assumed that the only audience that mattered was the scientific community, and that the only style that mattered was the scientific one familiar to that audience. But as Kroeber recognized at the time, this style limited the kinds of information that could be communicated; it also limited the audience that was willing and able to wade through it.

Life History

Because the idea of recounting one's autobiography is foreign to most cultures, and because the questions, editing, and explanations of the anthropologist so often guide and illuminate the narrative, the line between biography and autobiography becomes difficult to discern. The term *life history* has come to be employed by anthropologists as a substitute (Langness, 1965). For example, *Kiki:Ten Thousand Years in a Lifetime* (1968) was spoken into a tape recorder by Albert Maori Kiki, the author-subject. The tape was edited and there was some "rephrasing" and "restructuring" done by Ulli Beier, who had urged Kiki to record his life. Actually, the editing involved in this case is much less than in most. In some cases rather extensive notes have had to be added to life histories in order to render them more intelligible. Peter Nabokov, for example, in *Two Leggings: The Making of a*

Crow Warrior, reports that, "Without Robert Lowie's extensive work [ethnographic publications on the Crow] it would be impossible to interpret much of what Two Leggings recalls" (1967:xxi).

In such a situation where the life history is the work of at least two persons, one inside the culture and one outside of it, the question arises as to how much the document can be accepted as the product of the informant and his culture and how much it is a product of the anthropologist and his. In Linderman's life history of Plenty-coups, the Crow chief, the questions he asks have been inserted into the text so that one may judge how much was prompted by Linderman and how much was the subject's natural way of structuring his life. In addition, Linderman attempts to indicate the conditions under which the telling of the story occurred and the reactions of Plenty-coups, in the following instance, to his vision quest:

> Plenty-coups hesitated, his dimmed eyes staring over my head into the past. His last words, spoken in a whisper, had lifted him away. He had forgotten me and even the two old men who, like himself, appeared to be under a spell and scarcely breathed. (1930:70)

On other occasions, Plenty-coups was forgetful, bored, irritated, or distracted.

Information about the mood of one's informant is important in judging the significance of the facts being recounted and the probable biases which may have occurred in their telling. An anthropologist may have told his informant that he wanted to know about the old days; this stated wish might affect what the informant told him. The informant, in turn, wanting the anthropologist to have a high opinion of his culture, might then censor any facts which he felt were derogatory.

The life-history document is useful for studying cultural changes that have occurred over time. It also can be a way to learn about cultural deviance—what prompts acts of deviance and which consequences follow. Radin's life history of a Winnebago Indian, *Crashing Thunder*, is a good example. But the one thing which the life history does most excellently is to give a reader the insider's view of the culture; the life history captures not only the way that various cultural patterns come together and are linked in the life of an individual, but also their significance to him and his reactions to them in turn. This point of view is almost always missing from a standard ethnography.

The one point for the reader to keep in mind is that the life history is the work of only one person in the culture. It is subject to his distortions of memory and his bias in choosing what facts will be told. It is the document of an insider's view of his life, but only as he has chosen to reveal it.

Life histories have a strong appeal merely by their subject matter and the fact that they are presented in narrative form. When skillfully done, with the right subjects and the right editor, such works can be of great interest and importance. They can also be moving works of high quality. Consider the following comment by Jean-Paul Sartre (1970) on anthropologist Oscar Lewis's *The Children of Sanchez* (1961):

The Children of Sanchez is not a literary work, but it renders a mass of literary works redundant. Why write a novel on its characters or their milieu? They tell us much more by themselves, with a much greater self-understanding and eloquence.

Personal Accounts of Fieldwork

For many years, anthropologists shared their fieldwork experiences within a close circle of colleagues and friends, but did not include the general public. One of the first anthropologists to publish an account of fieldwork was Laura Bohannan, who wrote under the pseudonym of Elenore Smith Bowen. Her fictionalized depiction of her fieldwork in an African tribe, *Return to Laughter* (1954), caused something of a sensation in anthropological circles when it was first published. It has now become a classic, however, accepted by the profession, on the "must" reading list of many Departments of Anthropology, and held up to graduate students of anthropology as a masterful account of the process of doing fieldwork. David Riesman, in his Foreword to the 1964 Natural History Library edition, has written:

. . . For any assumption that an autobiography of affective experience is an ethnographic irrelevancy would, as I have argued earlier, be setting a wrong model for what is truly scientific. . . . As a work of ethnography, and as a primer of anthropological method, *Return to Laughter* can stand on its own feet. (1964:xvi)

It is interesting to note that Bohannan claims her work is fictitious:

All the characters in this book, except myself, are fictitious in the fullest meaning of that word. I knew people of the type I have described here; the incidents of the book are of the genre I myself experienced in Africa. Nevertheless, so much is fiction. I am an anthropologist. The tribe I have described here does exist. This book is the story of the way I did fieldwork among them. The ethnographic background given here is accurate, but it is neither complete nor technical. Here I have written simply as a human being, and the truth I have tried to tell concerns the sea change in oneself that comes from immersion in another and savage culture. (Author's Note, Laura Bohannan, 1964)

Despite Bohannan's note, readers seem to feel that there is a ring of truth in the experiences recounted; and no one, as far as we know, has attempted to distinguish just how much is fictional and how much is not.

The success of this book, among anthropologists, is remarkable when we consider that it was published during the very period when anthropologists most strongly professed their scientific aspirations. Perhaps the climate was becoming more favorable to an open discussion of matters of this sort (although Bohannan discreetly concealed her real identity for ten years). Anthropologists were beginning to recognize a need to analyze the techniques by which they actually gathered their field data. They also recognized a need to prepare and train students in a more rigorous fashion for their first fieldwork experience.

Since Bohannan's book, many other anthropologists have attempted to portray their fieldwork experience, including their relationships with key informants and others, in a way which conveys facts that would otherwise be unreported. Joseph B. Casagrande, in his introduction to *In the Company of Man*, has stated the concern as well as anyone:

> Field research is a challenging scientific undertaking, an adventure of both the mind and the spirit. It is also a memorable *human* experience, yet most anthropological writings tend to obscure the fact. Concerned with cultural patterns and norms, we are accustomed in articles and monographs to treat our data at a highly abstract level several stages removed from the vividness and immediacy of what we have experienced in the field. In our published work remarkably little is vouchsafed about personal reactions to the vicissitudes of field work and to the people among whom we have lived and worked. Most particularly, significant relationships with individuals who have been our close associates for many months are as a rule memorialized in a mere footnote or a few brief prefatory sentences.
>
> In this book we wish to share with the reader the personal experience of field work, and to communicate the essentially humane quality of our discipline in a way that is at once aesthetically, emotionally, and scientifically satisfying. (1960:xii)

In the Company of Man, a collection of articles about fieldwork, was a refreshing innovation in the presentation of anthropological materials. There have been several such attempts in recent years to do essentially the same thing (Freilich, 1970; Golde, 1970; Kimball and Watson, 1972; Spindler, 1970; Wax, 1971; Henry and Saberwal, 1969).

Accounts of fieldwork can have several functions. One function is to recreate for others the subjective reality of the field experience—the "sea changes," as Bohannan termed them, that are occasioned by crossing over into an alien culture to live. Such accounts allow others to share the investigator's plans, thoughts, feelings, and interpretations as he lives his daily life in another culture. They thus provide information about how his fieldwork was done and at the same time provide a glimpse of a strange culture through the eyes of a member of the reader's own culture—an aspect which is rarely discussed in most ethnographic monographs.

Some accounts of fieldwork are written primarily as ethnographies with the narrator himself a minor spectator. In these accounts, the aim is usually to capture the society in the round—to introduce the reader to individuals and the way they act out cultural patterns in daily life, embellishing them with their own flourishes and leaving their individual stamp upon their society.

Among those personal accounts intended primarily as ethnography, an early and lasting one is *The People of the Twilight* (1928), Diamond Jenness's description of two years with the Eskimo of the Coronation Gulf Region. In addition to the wealth of ethnographic information which it contains, there are anecdotes which share

(Drawing by Chas. Addams; © 1964 The New Yorker Magazine, Inc.)

with the reader some of the problems Jenness encountered in his fieldwork. At the same time, the individuals that he knew and the situations he observed are captured on paper in a naturalistic fashion which is missing from ethnographic monographs. A similar more recent account of experiences with the Eskimo from a female anthropologist's point of view is Jean L. Briggs's *Never in Anger* (1970).

Another valuable work is Francis Huxley's *Affable Savages, An Anthropologist among the Urubu Indians of Brazil* (1956). Huxley made abundant use of anecdotes in order "to show how Indians live and enjoy themselves: to show them, in fact, as subjects, not just as the objects of an anthropological study" (1956:16). He succeeds very well and gives not only an enjoyable reading experience but considerable ethnographic information as well.

Certainly one of the best of the books in this genre is Elizabeth Marshall Thomas's *The Harmless People* (1959), written about her experiences in the Kalahari Desert with the Bushmen. It is not only an extremely valuable ethnographic document, but also a highly literate one. As in the case of the Jenness book, the reader becomes intimately acquainted with several people as individuals and is able to understand something of why people behave as they do from their own point of view.

A book of similar quality is Colin Turnbull's *The Forest People: A Study of the Pygmies of the Congo* (1961). One criticism that might be leveled at this book is that it is too much of an "inside" picture, identifying so strongly with the Pygmies that Turnbull became somewhat ethnocentric toward the neighboring Bantu villagers. But as we noted earlier, Turnbull also wrote a full-scale standard ethnographic monograph, *Wayward Servants* (1965), which dispassionately provides ethnographic detail on all aspects of Pygmy culture.

A book that represents a more equal balance between personal experience and ethnographic description is K. E. Read's *The High Valley* (1965), a record of his fieldwork among the Gahuku people of New Guinea. Read stated the aim of his book this way:

> This record has been unequivocally subjective. I have hoped to convey something of the quality of Gahuku life—its color, its movement, the great occasions and the everyday events, even its smells, the personalities of its participants, the motives for their actions, and the landscape that formed their setting—as it appeared through my own eyes, filtered through my own background, my likes and dislikes, qualified by my own strengths and weakness. These are the two dimensions that were emphasized deliberately. (1965:247)

Read may regard this subjectivity as a confession of inadequacy. We see it instead as inevitable, and its explicit discussion as a great virtue. Read's book gives the reader a wealth of accurate ethnographic information; throughout the book the reader has little difficulty in determining what the author's subjective feelings are as contrasted with ethnographic fact. This book comes very close to demonstrating anthropology as an art form, but it also has clear scientific merit.

Interestingly, since Read wrote *The High Valley*, there has been an increased emergence of self-consciousness among ethnographers (Nash and Wintrob, 1972).

A work that demonstrates even more dramatically the importance to anthropology of personal, subjective accounts, as well as the advantages of presenting data in a different literary mode, is Carlos Castaneda's remarkable trilogy, *The Teachings of Don Juan: A Yaqui Way of Knowledge* (1968), *A Separate Reality* (1971), and *Journey to Ixtlan* (1972). These three volumes deal with the relationship between an anthropologist and his key informant. This particular relationship was far more complicated than most, involving as it did an anthropologist's sensitive attempt to understand something about an extraordinary Yaqui Indian who was a man at once of power, of knowledge, of sorcery, and of wisdom. As an account of fieldwork it is invaluable and interesting. As an ethnographic documentation of another way of knowledge it is, perhaps, priceless. The narrative descriptive style enables us to watch the progression of the relationship between Castaneda and Don Juan as instruction proceeds. It reveals Castaneda's thoughts and feelings as he undergoes this unusual indoctrination into another way of knowledge, telling something of the process whereby such rituals of instruction come to have a profound impact on the mind and emotions of an apprentice. There is a certain amount of controversy over the accuracy of some of Castaneda's materials, but the facts of this matter are not at issue here. What is important for our discussion is the form chosen to present this type of material. That Castaneda here made the best choice seems clear.

Innovative Forms of Presentation

One notable innovation is *Nine Dayak Nights* (1957) by W. R. Geddes. This piece of literature is designed to transcend cultural boundaries by taking a form which reflects the intellectual, moral, and aesthetic themes of the culture it is attempting to describe. The description takes the form of a long story which is told by the Dayaks themselves. Parts of the story are sung, parts are told, and parts are acted. We find a peculiar land of magical deeds, giants, dragons, love, murder, and war. The story points up particularly well the different (from Geddes's) view of morality that the Dayaks have. The story takes nine nights to complete and, when told, has managed to convey a quantity of ethnographic information to the reader, besides offering considerable insight into the attitudes and thought processes of the Dayaks.

Behind Mud Walls 1930-1960 (1969), by the missionaries William and Charlotte Wiser, combines a more or less straightforward ethnographic description with extensive use of quotations from the people themselves.

Some idea of the richness of this approach may be seen in the following brief example:

To a newcomer we may seem suspicious, obstinate, intolerant, backward—everything that goes with refusal to change. We did not choose these characteristics for ourselves. Experience forced them upon our fathers. And the warnings of our fathers, added to our own experiences, have drilled them into us. Refusal to change is the armor with which we have learned to protect ourselves. If we and our fathers had accepted the new ideas and customs commended to us, we might have made greater progress. But greater progress would have drawn the eyes of a covetous world toward us. And then our lot would have been worse than before. Where are the cities that flourished for a time? In ruins. While they climbed to great heights and fell to the depths of destruction we kept to the old reliable level. And we have survived. We are not blind to the advantages of the new, but unless we know just where it will lead us, we prefer to let it pass by. (1969:118)

Another book that needs to be mentioned is Jules Henry's *Jungle People* (1941). It is an unusual and instructive example not only because of Henry's claim that it was the first anthropological monograph written from a psychoanalytic point of view but also because he insisted it must have a plot. His remarks on this plot feature are of great interest although they seem not to have influenced other anthropologists to any great extent:

Jungle People has a plot because the life of the Kaingáng has one. Yet, since behavioral science views life as plotless, *Jungle People* violates an underlying premise. Moreover, in the behavioral sciences, to state that life not only has a plot but must be described as if it did is like spitting in church.

The conception of culture as plotless has a long and respectable history in American anthropology and is supported by all respectable departments. Even Ruth Benedict's *Patterns of Culture* and *The Chrysanthemum and the Sword*, however eloquently they have presented the theme of plot in culture, have not been able to overcome the entrenched respectability of plotlessness. One can understand why this should be, for a determined search for meaning in life confronts us eventually with the fact that many of its meanings are delusive. The search for meaning and plot in culture ultimately compels one to look for them in his own life, and since this may lead to despair, it is better not to search at all. Hence in cultural anthropology "integration" and "function" have been substituted for plot, and anthropology has been made safe. (1964:xvii)

In another innovative technique, Walter Goldschmidt has attempted to record a significant cultural encounter in its totality (1969, 1972). Such detailed narrative description bears some resemblance to the tape-recording technique of Oscar Lewis and is similar to detailed techniques of recording that have been developed in ethology, psychology, and sociology. When Kambuya—a wealthy cattle owner among the Sebei of Uganda—died, a network of kinsmen met to liquidate his estate. With the help of an interpreter, Goldschmidt attempted to record these proceedings in their entirety. Although some of the action, which extended over many days, took place in Goldschmidt's absence, and some of what was witnessed was misheard or misrecorded, Goldschmidt believes that he nevertheless captured an accurate and complete record of the event. To record a significant event (a funeral, marriage, or religious ceremony) in such complete detail is not unique in fieldwork; anthropologists often attempt to make such records. Goldschmidt's innovation comes in *presenting* the event in its full detail. In addition to the transcript itself, Goldschmidt provides interpretations and annotations to clarify or expand upon various passages. The following brief excerpt illustrates the kind of detailed conversation that this style of presentation provides:

Mwanga: Gentlemen, may I know whether my friendship is finished now that Kambuya is dead?

Ndiwa V: Please, Mwanga, do not be roundabout—just speak frankly. I know that you are claiming a cow for crying.

Ndiwa: You have been saying that Mwanga should receive a cow.

Ndiwa V: (addressing Ndiwa): Before Salimu was back, you said that Mwanga should be given a cow.

Ndiwa: No, I did not say that; I said that we should wait till Salimu comes back.

Salimu: It is very difficult to give this man a cow; if we do so, members of our clan who have been claiming the same and who have received no cow will hear about it, and we shall receive bitter complaints. Therefore, I would suggest that Ndiwa and I each give him 50 shillings instead. (1969:148-149)

In his comments about this exchange (which, of course, requires that the speakers and their relationships be known) Goldschmidt explains that whereas everyone would soon know about any payment in the form of an animal—where after all could it be hidden?—that money could be exchanged surreptitiously. We see clearly how individuals behave within the rules of their culture, but we see also how they use these rules to their own advantage.

Since this approach involves no generalization at all, it is clearly not efficient; an entire book is required to report a single event. However, the approach is useful in giving the reader a glimpse of real life as it is spoken and acted by people who are engaged in a dramatic and meaningful episode in their lives. Such a document can be most revealing, and can serve well to complement other more standard styles of ethnographic presentation.

Still another technique to be considered appears in the attempts by various anthropologists to describe a culture as it might have been in the past or at the time of first contact with Europeans. This technique requires a great deal of historical reconstruction and is fraught with the dangers that accompany all such speculations. Paul Radin used this technique in his prologue to *The Story of the American Indian* (1927b). It has been used more recently by Gene Weltfish (*The Lost Universe*, 1965) and by the Aginskys (*Deep Valley*, 1967). It is also the technique employed in part by Pat Ritzenthaler in *The Fon of Bafut* (1966).

Finally, perhaps the most innovative and interesting way yet attempted to present ethnographic information is Hilda Kuper's marvelous play about witchcraft, *A Witch in My Heart* (1970), set in Swaziland in the 1930's. It conveys the drama, emotion, and strains associated with acts of witchcraft in a way that far transcends the printed word. The ethnographic merit of this work, along with its over-all merit as a play, can be seen in the fact that it has been produced in Swazi schools. So far, this is the only attempt of its kind by an anthropologist. Kuper had previously written a fine ethnographic novel, *Bite of Hunger* (1965). Her comments on writings of this kind are well worth noting:

> . . . because the artist as well as the anthropologist or any other being is part of the world in which she lives, she remains partly grounded by the conventions of that world. It marks and limits her imagination so that even the world of creation is never completely culture free and boundless. At the same time the "discoveries" of anthropologists, as well as of astronauts and other adventurers, have already extended the horizon of writers of fiction, and provided artists with new insights and new imagery.
>
> The drama, the novel, the poem, and the monograph complement one another, each presenting a different facet of the whirling worlds around and within the self. (1970:xi)

Ethnographic Films

Ethnographic films have been criticized as research tools because they are so time-consuming to analyze and so costly to make. But as means of presenting ethnographic information they are of undeniable value. Such films as *Nanook of the North* (Flaherty, 1922), the first such film ever made about the lives of the Eskimo; *The Hunters* (Marshall and Gardner, 1956), about the Bushmen; and *Dead Birds* (Gardner, 1964), about the Dani of New Guinea are valuable records of behavior in these societies. They, and other films like them, allow us to visualize the physical environment, the features and dress of the people, their adornment, their grace and tempo, their ways of sitting, talking, working, hunting, and fighting. These films serve, that is, to bring to life what we have previously read about and imagined only imperfectly.

Other films do more than this because they show us something so foreign to our experience that reading about it, especially in the standard monograph, is a wholly inadequate means of comprehension. Take Peter Adair's (1967) film, *The Holy Ghost People*, about a fundamentalist snake-handling cult in West Virginia. Weston LaBarre (1969) has written a skillful account of these people; how they congregate to cure by beseeching God, how they dance and sing, go into trances, fall down in convulsions, speak in tongues, handle deadly rattlesnakes and copperheads, and drink strychnine. They are a dramatic people to read about and LaBarre writes about them well, but actually seeing them is something altogether different. The fervor is visible—starkly so. Their convulsions appear to be stereotyped yet at the same time they are violent and frightening. The trances are impressive, and along with the accompanying music, are compellingly infectious. Speaking in tongues, when witnessed in this way, no longer seems grotesque or merely clinical; it is fascinating and serious. The snakes are terrifyingly real. When one snake eventually bites the minister, his fear and confusion are communicated to us in a shocking denouement. The strange is suddenly real, and frightening and puzzling in a way that few artists could achieve in a book.

A similar example is the Australian Aboriginal practice of subincision. This surgical operation was performed over much of the desert area of Australia, and many written accounts of its details are available in the literature. We know from these accounts that teen-age boys underwent this operation as part of a cycle of ceremonies of great supernatural significance. We know that a stone knife was used to cut the urethra open from the scrotum to the glans while the initiate was required to lie impassively; any undue display of fear or pain led to his execution. We even have a variety of explanations telling us why the ritual was performed. All of this information is intriguing and dramatic. Once again, however, to witness subincision done is something altogether different. Australian anthropologist Norman Tindale (1937) filmed subincision among the Pitjandjara tribe in the late 1930's. His black-and-white film records the ceremony from start to finish. We see tension-building preliminaries, close-up shots of the cutting being done, and a paralyzing picture of one boy who showed his pain. The boy, we are told, was later put to death. It is difficult to imagine any artist, however great, who could describe these scenes with an impact similar to the one Tindale put on celluloid.

Eventually people in the societies anthropologists study will make their own films, like the books they are already writing (Achebe, 1959; Eri, 1970; Laye, 1959, for example) to tell us still more about their lives as they see them. In the meantime, we expect to see ethnographic films develop in sophistication as means for presenting certain aspects of life that written media cannot do as well. It is a curious fact of contemporary anthropology, however, that ethnographic films, which so obviously involve selection, editing, often deliberate acting and other distortions of reality, are so eagerly and widely accepted by the public, novels and even personal accounts of fieldwork are not.

Conclusion

What we know of other peoples has come to us almost entirely by way of the printed page. The ethnographic monograph has its role in providing anthropologists with their basic data for an understanding of man. The other ethnographic styles we have discussed, however, have a wider appeal. Because they introduce a naturalistic mode of descriptive narration, they more closely reflect real life. People have always been curious about how people in other cultures live, and the general public readily takes up such books as *The Children of Sanchez* (Lewis, 1961), *Ishi in Two Worlds* (T. Kroeber, 1961), and *The Teachings of Don Juan* (Castaneda, 1968), to make them bestsellers. These alternative literary forms speak in a way that allows the reader to be swept up in the action—to think, feel, and experience vicariously what life is like for persons in another culture. Because the reader is caught up emotionally, however, it is even more important that he be aware of the possible distortions that can find their way into such writing.

The crux of the dispute over science and humanism, ethnographic monographs and other forms of presentation, should not rest on the question of whether or not it is professional to write a popular work; anthropologists more and more recognize the value of sharing their understandings of other cultures with a wider audience. Instead, the debate should center on the issue of how best to convey information about life in other cultures. The standard monograph conveys one dimension of life. Other styles of presenting ethnographic information convey different, and equally important, understandings about life in other cultures. In judging these various styles, the reader must ask, first, how the information presented helps to fill out our understanding of man and culture, and, second, whether the information presented is accurate. However much debate there may be about the first, all anthropologists agree about the second. Anthropologists, although perfectly capable of error like everyone else, always attempt to give unbiased accounts of other people in so far as that goal is possible. They attempt to show how even the seemingly bizarre and extreme usually contains something of value—that the customs of others have a consistency and dignity however much they differ from our own. If anthropologists have not always succeeded in this task, their attempts nevertheless stand in sharp contrast to the distorted, commercialized, and sensationalized writing of those whose interest is not truth and understanding but political or financial gain.

As the world is becoming smaller and as it becomes increasingly necessary for its various peoples to understand each other and get along together, it becomes more imperative that the information we receive about each other be both correct and sensitively conveyed. Thus it becomes crucial for each person to read and to study with a fuller awareness the problems both of finding out about others and of what can happen to ethnographic content as it responds to style and intention. Along these lines, consider finally a quotation from John Hospers:

> We are probably convinced that the novels of Balzac give us a reasonably accurate picture of certain aspects of life in Paris in the early nineteenth century, that in fact they were intended to do this; but whether or not they were so intended, they do. Yet we do not encounter, on reading any of these, any sentence such as "this is a true picture of life in Paris in my time: I do hereby assert it." (1960:39)

Balzac did not assert it, it would seem obvious, because it was only incidental to his main motive for writing, whatever that may have been—fortune, fame, entertainment, edification, or compulsion. Anthropologists have motives that go beyond the mere presentation of ethnographic fact, it is true; but the one thing that should distinguish the anthropologist as an ethnographic writer is precisely that he does and must preface his work, however implicitly: "This is a true picture—I do hereby assert it."

Further Readings

There is no single work that deals with the issue of styles of reporting in anthropology. We must here simply mention titles, repeating many we have already mentioned. As examples of the range of "standard monographs" see Boas's *The Central Eskimo* (1888), Evans-Pritchard's *The Nuer* (1940), Malinowski's *Argonauts of the Western Pacific* (1922), Firth's *We the Tikopia* (1957), Hogbin's *The Island of Menstruating Men* (1970), Mead's *Coming of Age in Samoa* (1928), Leach's *Pul Eliya: A Village in Ceylon* (1961), Lewis's *Life in a Mexican Village* (1951), Bunzel's *Chichicastenango* (1959), DuBois's *The People of Alor* (1961), Nadel's *A Black Byzantium* (1942), Radcliffe-Brown's *The Andaman Islanders* (1948), and Opler's *An Apache Life Way* (1965).

Ethnographic novels include *The Delight Makers* by Adolph Bandelier (1890), *Flesh of the Wild Ox: A Riffian Chronicle of High Valleys and Long Rifles* by Carleton Coon (1932), Robert Ekvall's *Tents Against the Sky*, Freuchen's *Eskimo* (1931), Hilda Kuper's *Bite of Hunger* (1965), Peter Matthiessen's *Under the Mountain Wall* (1962), Ruth Underhill's *Hawk over Whirlpools* (1940), *The Golden Wing* by Lin Yueh-hwa (1947), and LaFarge's famous *Laughing Boy* (1929).

The most interesting personal accounts of anthropological fieldwork include Bowen/Bohannan's *Return to Laughter* (1954/1964), Briggs's *Never in Anger*, Castaneda's *The Teachings of Don Juan* (1968), *A Separate Reality* (1971), and *Journey to Ixtlan* (1972), Fernea's *Guests of the Sheik* (1965), Gazaway's *The Longest Mile* (1969), Huxley's *Affable Savages* (1956), Jenness's *The People of the Twilight* (1928), the collection *Crossing Cultural Boundaries* edited by Kimball and Watson (1972), Levi-Strauss's well-known *A World on the Wane* (1961; *Tristes Tropiques*, 1955). Hortense Powdermaker's *Stranger and Friend*, Read's *The High Valley* (1965), Elizabeth Thomas's *The Harmless People* (1959), Turnbull's *The Forest People* (1961), and, perhaps, Yoors's *The Gypsies* (1967).

For the use of life histories by anthropologists see *The Life History in Anthropological Sciences* by Langness (1965). For some better than average life histories see Oscar Lewis's *The Children of Sanchez* (1961) and *Pedro Martinez* (1964); Nabokov's *Two Leggings: The Making of a Crow Warrior* (1967); Pat Ritzenthaler's *The Fon of Bafut* (1966); Stands-in-Timber and Liberty, *Cheyenne Memories* (1967); Sugihara and Plath, *Sensei and his People: The Building of a Japanese Commune* (1969); and Margery Wolf's *The House of Lim* (1968).

Some novels of ethnographic interest not written by anthropologists include Pearl Buck's *The Good Earth* (1931), *In Cold Blood* by Truman Capote (1965), *The Timeless Land* by Eleanor Dark (1941), James Houston's *The White Dawn* (1971), Aubrey Menen's *A Prevalence of Witches* (1948), Josephina Niggli's *Mexican Village* (1945), and A. E. Wells's *Men of the Honey Bee* (1971).

There is a variety of other works that attempt to portray ethnographic materials in distinctive ways. *American Indian Life*, edited by Parsons (1922), was such an attempt. Freuchen's *Book of the Eskimo* (1961) contains a number of short pieces and short stories. Geddes's *Nine Dayak Nights* (1957) is a unique attempt to present materials in story form; and Jules Henry's *Jungle People* (1941) is supposed to be an ethnographic monograph with a plot. Hilda Kuper, in addition to her novel and short stories, has also written a play, *A Witch in My Heart* (1970).

For ethnographic films, of which there is a continually growing number, see *Films for Anthropological Teaching*, edited by Karl Heider (1972). For a discussion of how they are made see *Exploring the Film* by William Kuhns and Robert Stanley (1968), and Collier's *Visual Anthropology* (1967).

PART III EXPLANATION AND CROSS-CULTURAL COMPARISON

Each anthropologist's fieldwork in a society is his contribution to a store of knowledge about societies all over the world. To seek an understanding of man and his culture, the ultimate goal of anthropology, requires stepping back from the intimate inspection of life in one society and making a broad comparison of life in a great many societies. The work of cross-cultural comparison is vital to anthropology. *Ethnography*, or the description of cultures, provides the raw materials. Cross-cultural comparison is the use of these materials to test various hypotheses about man and culture. Only by such tests of theory can our understanding of man and culture progress. Therefore in this Part III we will discuss the methods that anthropologists use to perform this important task, the difficulties that they encounter in formulating their hypotheses for cross-cultural comparison, and the problems they face in determining the significance of their results.

Social and economic conditions tend to mold the intellectual climate of a period and through it the theories put forth about the nature of man, culture, and society. These theories, in turn, influence students of man, anthropologists included. They guide the choice of the data which are collected and the uses to which they are put. For example, in a period in which man is thought to act primarily for economic gain, attention may turn toward the economic sector of society. The methods might emphasize counting and the translation of various acts into units of economic equivalence. Less interest might be given to the aesthetic, play-loving, and gregarious aspects of man's behavior. Or if, instead, the sexual aspect of man's nature is held to dominate his behavior, attention might turn instead, as it did with Freud, to the biosexual development of the human animal, to the repression of his basic sexuality, and to the social and cultural consequences of such repression.

It is important to keep in mind that beliefs change about the nature of man and the nature of culture. Theories of one age are replaced by theories of the next. These changes are accompanied by changes in the questions that anthropologists ask, in the facts that are gathered, in the methods of gathering and handling them, and in the types of causal explanations which are made.

Anthropologists have sought various explanations for man and his culture. Early evolutionists believed that societies progressed through cultural stages from savagery to civilization—societies with different cultural patterns were in different stages of evolution, progressing to a new stage when increased knowledge permitted them to devise "better" and more "efficient" customs to replace their old ones. This was the evolutionists' explanation of the origin of various customs. For instance, Lewis Henry Morgan, who was interested in social organization, proposed that in the earliest stage of organized society all the men and women of a group shared each other equally in a group marriage. As the dangerous effects of such inbreeding with brothers and sisters became apparent to them, however, they gradually prohibited such marriages and passed to the next stage in which groups of brothers held wives in common or groups of sisters shared husbands. The accumulation of ethnographic evidence failed to support these somewhat simplistic schemes of universal progression, and the evolutionists' designation of Western European culture as the high point came to be considered arbitrary, to say the least.

Evolutionary explanation was followed by attempts to show that cultural practices were originated by one or more highly inventive societies and then spread or "diffused" by borrowing and migration to other societies around the world. Because diffusion was slow, societies near the centers of origin always had newer and "better" customs while those farther away had older and "less advanced" ones. This explanation often rested on a speculative reconstruction of the history of many preliterate societies and thus was not open to direct proof.

Other anthropologists sought the causes of cultural phenomena in the nature of social systems themselves, contending that each cultural practice should be explained by demonstrating the role it played in maintaining the system of which it was a part. Others emphasized the ways in which cultural practices also met man's basic biological and psychological needs. Still others traced cultural forms to technological and economic factors. These explanations, and others like them, directed attention to the nature of man, culture, and society, and to the forces that influenced them.

However well anthropologists may call attention to patterns of cultural behavior in one society, anthropology's ultimate goal is the understanding of man in all societies, a goal which can only be accomplished by making cross-cultural comparison. Cross-cultural comparison involves a search for regularities in man's cultural behavior. But even more important, it is a search for wider theories of human behavior which bind these regularities together and provide an understanding of how and why cultures take the forms that they do.

A cross-cultural comparison may require asking in how many societies there is a belief in a pleasant afterworld or in how many societies men may marry several wives at once, but the cross-cultural analysis does not stop with answers to these questions. Cross-cultural comparison is an attempt to explain *why* some societies have certain beliefs about religion or marriage while others have quite different ones, and then to extend that explanation by searching for a more general understanding of human religious behavior or human sexual behavior. Anthropologists who employ this form of comparison look for generalizations—or laws—that hold for men in *any* society. Because cross-cultural comparison is the method by which anthropology tries out its theories of man and culture, one must understand the process by which this difficult task is accomplished. First, we must consider some aspects of comparison itself.

Comparing Human Behavior

The cultural patterns of societies, when placed side by side and compared, are like the patterns of snowflakes in that no two are exactly alike. Yet a discerning eye can find similarities between aspects of one pattern and aspects of another. The unique and the similar reside in each event of the everyday world. Depending on how the observer looks at the event, he may consider it different from anything which has ever happened before, or he may note its similarities to other events. Thus an anthropologist could attend a thousand birthday parties in our society and find variations of detail which made each party unique. The words of a toast to a young "birthday boy," the fact that one celebrant is over 100 years old, and the gag gift of a mink-lined bathtub received by a wealthy celebrant may variously be unique among those thousand parties. But if the anthropologist looked he could also find similarities in each of the thousand birthday parties, such as the fact that at each party guests were invited, that a birthday cake was served as part of the menu, that candles on the cake were blown out while the celebrant made a wish, and that presents were opened by the one being honored.

Recognizing the similarities and differences in events is necessary in order to make predictions about human behavior. The anthropologist's search for laws of human behavior is an endeavor to identify which forces and conditions produce similar human behavior, which produce variations of these behaviors, and which produce quite different behaviors altogether, and then to specify how these forces act and interact. Man's confidence that the events of the natural world follow laws that he can discover is the belief on which all science is built. Anthropologists have attempted to build their science by comparing human cultural behavior and searching for the underlying conditions that will explain man and culture.

When the anthropologist draws a portrait of a living society in his ethnography, he recognizes the uniqueness of the day-to-day events he has seen, but he extracts similarities from them in order to reveal the underlying cultural pattern. In the older ethnographies it is usual to find that the description is either a report of what should ideally happen or else of modal behavior—what typically happens. For example, the Plains Indians were renowned for their ability as warriors. They extolled the brave warrior and their men typically lived up to the ideal. There was a variation of this pattern, however; some men were so far incapable of such bravado that they took on the role of women and stayed out of warfare altogether. More recent ethnographies continue to give recognition to data on ideal patterns and modal patterns, but they also attempt to discuss less frequent variations. With descriptions like these in hand, an outsider can make fairly accurate predictions about what people in a particular society will do in a given situation. These descriptions contain regularities, or rules, that apply to one society. Within a single society, as we have indicated previously, the anthropologist may also venture to explain "why" a particular cultural form originated, proposing an explanation based implicitly on his general notions about how all human societies work. This explanation must usually remain unsubstantiated, however, unless it is tested further in more societies. This is one limitation of study within a single society.

Another limitation grows from the fact that predictions based on events witnessed in only one society often do not take account of new conditions which arise in that society to produce new forms; the process of cultural change is continual in the history of any culture. An example is the sexual revolution in America, which in the past ten years has changed attitudes toward premarital sexual relations and brought greater openness to many other areas of sexual behavior which were formerly taboo in our society. If the anthropologist is to understand and to predict new cultural forms which may arise, he must discover which forms *can* occur and under what conditions they can occur. To do this, he must step outside the confines of one culture to view the range of cultural variation occurring in other societies.

The Development of Cross-Cultural Comparison

Anthropology as a discipline was born in the heyday of evolutionary theories. Applied to man, these theories boldly proposed that man's culture had evolved through a series of grades from "lower" barbaric forms to "higher" more civilized ones. The exotic and alien customs of societies around the world became building material for anthropological theorists. Because cross-cultural comparison was the accepted procedure for discovering and testing hypotheses derived from these theories, the customs and institutions of various societies were sorted and classified and assigned to different evolutionary stages. Yet, as we have mentioned, all this work did not lead to an illumination of the laws of culture. Cross-cultural comparison does not automatically produce the discovery of laws. First, the ethnographic evidence must be accurate and complete. Further, the law seeker must have a theory that allows the facts to be put together in such a way that they lead to understanding. The ethnographic information available in these early days was not always accurate, and the theories were not always useful. Thus no amount of comparison could lead to valid explanations.

The period of optimistic attempts to set forth laws of cultural behavior using materials gleaned mainly from the accounts of travelers and missionaries gave way to a period in which anthropologists themselves undertook fieldwork. American anthropologists, led by Boas, were skeptical of many of the evolutionists' theoretical pronouncements, and they sought to collect the evidence which would disprove them. Some anthropologists emphasized the integrity of each culture's pattern, in which all the parts interlocked to make a meaningful whole. They felt that none of these parts could be torn from context for purposes of comparison without causing a serious distortion. Cross-cultural comparison therefore withered, and Boas himself finally confessed to doubts that laws of cultural behavior could ever be found.

It is true, as many Boasians claimed, that all classifications "distort" to some degree by ignoring certain unique facets of the events they group together, but a good classification is one that draws attention to significant shared features which prove useful for gaining an understanding of how cultural systems work. Most anthropologists today believe that cross-cultural comparison is not only possible but also essential.

British anthropologists doing fieldwork during the same period were impressed, just as the Americans were, with the way in which the parts of a culture interlocked and seemed to accommodate themselves to each other rather like the parts of a machine or an organism. These anthropologists were called *functionalists* because they attempted to explain the existence of a particular cultural practice in the society they were studying by pointing out the social "function" or need that the practice fulfilled in helping to maintain the social system. Functionalists' explanations of particular practices were tailored to the cultural system of one particular society; with a few notable exceptions, no attempts were made to test these propositions outside that one society. This form of explanation gives rise to a dilemma. Functionalists claim that a practice exists because there is a need for it. In turn, the need is shown to exist because the presence of the practice indicates that it must. The reasoning is circular and therefore cannot be considered a proof (Hempel, 1959).

For example, Malinowski's fieldwork with the Trobriand Islanders convinced him that the function of ritual was to reduce the anxiety that people felt on various occasions. However, he could only assume the presence of anxiety just as he could only assume that ritual reduced it. In fact, other functionalists, including Radcliffe-Brown, came to quite different conclusions about the function of ritual.

The inability of the Boasians to find cultural laws and to solve the problems with functional explanations led to a slow revolution in the way anthropologists came to think about "causes," "explanations," and methods used in trying to understand man's culture. Anthropologists began to align themselves with the techniques and the philosophy of the natural sciences and to become again more generalizing and comparative, less tied to particularistic descriptions and explanations of life in one culture. Aided by the growth of computer technology, they were able to develop new methods for use in making cross-cultural comparisons of a large number of societies. Comparison enabled them to test their explanations of the influence of such factors as environmental conditions, child-rearing practices, or technological knowledge on various other aspects of culture, in order to produce better theories about man and culture.

Cultural anthropologists do not study human beings in laboratories. Instead they study man as he lives under natural conditions, and they use cross-cultural comparison and analysis to replace the controlled conditions and experimental procedures that other scientists achieve in their laboratories.

The Methods of Cross-Cultural Comparison

Most anthropologists are intrigued by all aspects of man's behavior, but the cross-cultural investigator must narrow his focus to a particular target problem if he hopes to gain mastery over the complexity of circumstances and interacting variables that entangle human behavior. His first step, and perhaps the most crucial, is to ask an important question.

All the sciences have gone forward when they have asked important, perhaps original, questions that were answerable. Asking a worthwhile question is difficult, and a field may stagnate while its scholars continue to ask minor variations of the traditional questions they learned as students. A good question is the result of skillful construction based on thorough knowledge of the field plus creative insight as to how such a question may be answered. Above all, a good question is one whose answer provides information relevant to more general theories about man and culture.

For example, human beings today are horrified by the possibility that another world war may end mankind and destroy all life on earth. Concerned persons might ask an anthropologist whether such annihilation is likely to be man's fate. The anthropologist could not predict the future, but he could set out to draft a question whose answer might lead at least part of the way toward an understanding of the problem. He might ask, "Under what conditions does man make war on man?" His underlying assumption might be the following: "Making war is not an automatic and inherent response in man; it is not just part of his nature or of his species behavior; therefore war must be a result of certain social and cultural conditions that can be identified." These questions might well be the preliminary steps in a difficult and enormously challenging assignment.

Operationalizing

Part of translating a question into a proposition for proof or plan for action is to define clearly what all the words in the proposition mean. It sometimes surprises newcomers to anthropology and other social sciences when they discover that they and others have not only the right but also the obligation to define their words as they wish and to tell others how they intend to use them. "Operationalizing" is the term for making such definitions because the scientist sets down the operations or the rules which, when followed, allow anyone else to recognize, classify, or measure things in precisely the same way he has done it.

War might seem to be a term that could be simply defined. One could start by going to a dictionary where he might find the following main definition:

War: a contest between nations or states (international war), or between parties in the same state (civil war), carried on by force of arms for various purposes, as to settle disputes about territorial possessions, to maintain rights that have been interfered with, to resist oppression, to avenge injuries, to conquer territory, to extend dominion, etc.; a conflict of arms between hostile parties or nations; open hostility declared or engaged in.

In the second alternative of this definition, the anthropologist finds a phrase which bothers him—"between parties in the same state." Intuitively, he would like to exclude from "war" an all-out brawl with fists and baseball bats that occurred one Saturday evening after the Smith family complained to neighbors about excessive drunkenness and noise. Do these families constitute two "parties?" How large is a "party?" If the anthropologist were to retain this dictionary's definition of war, he would have to include a set of directions for deciding what constitutes "a party." And still other terms would be open to various interpretations, such as "nation," "state," "force of arms," and so forth.

Anthropologists themselves have contributed a definition of warfare which is quite short—"armed combat between political communities" (Otterbein, 1972). Part of the work of operationalizing the term *war* is to decide which events or behaviors it is important to include under this term. The anthropological definition (aside from the fact that the term *political community* would need further clarification) would appear to exclude the bloody feuds of the Hatfields and McCoys as quarrels between families who were technically parts of a larger political unit. It might also refuse to acknowledge the initial fighting between the North and the South as a war on the reasoning that both sides were originally of one political unit. Definitions invariably run into problems such as those, which must be resolved before the research can continue.

The definition is the anthropologist's declaration of what he feels it is important to study. With this definition in hand, others may replicate his work, or may dispute it by showing that he has ignored significant points, but they will not be in doubt as to his use of his terms and he will not waste time in confused arguments arising merely because someone else thought he meant something by *war* which he did not.

Making Hypotheses: Beginning the Search for Evidence

Deciding what kinds of evidence to collect calls upon the ingenuity of the investigator in acting as a detective. For instance, geologists must gather their evidence on the conditions and forces which shaped the earth in the distant past from the stories they read out of the rocks and from their observations about the working of nature in the present. Anthropologists, like other scientists, must often take the evidence that is available to them rather than that which they would consider most conclusive; but an anthropologist who devises a new way to wring evidence from the ethnographic record may be able to answer a question that has remained long unsolved.

There are several strategies for collecting evidence but all involve some theory or idea that the anthropologist possesses for deciding which are likely to be the important factors involved. He may have had a flash of insight that war and some other factor, perhaps the possession of a military organization, were related. He might then ask the question, "Is the presence of some kind of military organization the condition that leads man eventually to make war?" He may believe that a "yes" answer to this question would make a good hypothesis because his reading of the ethnographic record has suggested to him that societies which lack formal military organizations (organizations such as camps of young warriors, warrior societies, or armies) do not engage in warfare.

Having decided upon the general question to be answered and having defined the necessary terms, the investigator must formulate the hypothesis. The hypothesis should state a proposition in such a form that it can be tested and then either confirmed or rejected. Hypotheses usually propose that a relationship exists between two factors which are known as *variables*; they are called variables because they change or vary according to the conditions present in a situation. In our example on warfare, the variables are *warfare* and *military organizations*. A positive form of the hypothesis might go as follows: "Warfare is more likely to occur in societies that have military organizations than in societies that lack such organizations." Whatever form the hypothesis takes, it must be clearly stated and there must be evidence available which can serve to test the relationship it states.

However much the anthropologist may believe that this hypothesis is a good one, he would be wise to entertain other hypotheses for at least two very important reasons. First, such an apparently self-evident linking of factors is unlikely to have been overlooked by others. If matters are really so simple, why did no one else reach this conclusion much earlier? The second reason is more fundamental. The anthropologist may indeed show that war and presence of a military organization are linked, but it is always possible for others to claim, "Oh yes, war and military organizations are highly correlated, but war may sometimes occur without the presence of a military organization, and even when it occurs with a military organization, it may be the presence of other factors that actually brings about war. Unless you have investigated these other factors, I will not consider your explanation very seriously." In essence, this critic of the anthropologist is telling him that even though he may be able to show that his two variables are highly *correlated* (mutually related), he must not assume that they are therefore in a causal relationship—that it is the presence of a military organization which *causes* warfare or of warfare which *causes* military organizations. A correlation between traits does not necessarily imply causality. Both traits could have been produced by a third, more basic factor, such as disputes over valuable resources or population crowding.

Because of the possible influence of the so-called "third factor," the cautious anthropologist entertains all of the alternative hypotheses that he believes to be reasonable. For example, he may test the correlation of warfare with various conditions of scarcity to see if societies have turned to war to gain new land or tribute which will enable them to maintain their standard of living. He may test whether warfare is correlated with inequalities in the distribution of resources among neighboring societies which would lead them to build military organizations to either defend or obtain these valuable resources. Or he may ask if warfare is correlated with a situation in which societies of approximately equal size are neighbors; their mere closeness and presence may invite disputes which could quickly escalate to warfare, given the fact that each society considers that it has at least an even chance to win. He cannot entertain every conceivable alternative hypothesis or he would never finish his task, but if he cannot justify the rejection of theoretically reasonable alternative hypotheses he cannot hope to convince anyone that his own hypothesis has value. The investigator's background knowledge of anthropology helps guide him in selecting significant factors and aids him in making hypotheses. At this point, he might even decide that the important characteristics involved in warfare vary with the type of war, and that it would be useful to classify his general concept of war into subtypes according to goals or procedures, and to classify the participants as aggressors or defenders.

In a complex situation such as warfare, many factors may be involved and interacting. Among the factors the anthropologist might deem important to examine and make hypotheses about are population size and carrying capacity of the land, subsistence pattern, type of leadership, type of political unit, kinds of competition and contact between units, form of military organization, type and location of important resources, relative size of the two units fighting, number of males in the population, level of war technology, various goals of warfare, and the participants' definitions of concepts such as "rights," "oppression," and "injuries." The investigator might also run through all his descriptions of warfare and sort out any additional variables that seemed significant or recurred frequently. He would then need to classify and make operational definitions for his variables, so that the relationship of each to the occurrence of warfare could be measured.

As the eminent philosopher of science, Karl Popper, has pointed out, no one can ever prove the truth of an assertion beyond a shadow of a doubt. It is always conceivable that somewhere in the world there is evidence which, if brought forward, might serve to disprove it. Since it is possible to disprove an assertion, sciences advance by eliminating hypotheses. Those which cannot be disproved and thereby eliminated *may* be true. The anthropologist should therefore construct his hypotheses in such a way that he can not only gather evidence which will tend to confirm them, but can also gather evidence which could disprove them.

The kinds of evidence that the anthropologist decides he is likely to find in the ethnographic record of other societies, combined with his preferred mode of collecting evidence, will guide his choice of how many and which societies he will use to study his problem. The selection of such societies is the next problem he must face.

Selecting Societies for Cross-Cultural Comparison

Selecting a few well-described societies which offer evidence supporting one's hypothesis is an appealing technique that has lured many anthropologists to use it. As a means of building strong confirmation for a hypothesis, though, it is unsatisfactory. Finding such a relationship or correlation between factors (let us say warfare and military organizations) in only two or three societies could mean very little; any number of factors, including historical accident, could have combined to produce a relationship known to exist in only three societies. Besides the fact that the weight of numbers will hardly be convincing, there is the problem that one cannot learn which one or more of the variables found to co-occur with a practice is actually responsible for maintaining it. For example, an investigator might choose to compare three societies in which warfare is found to be associated with patrilineal institutions, a strong ethic of male valor and bravery in battle, the practice of female infanticide, and an economy based on hunting of large game over wide areas—four variables. Which of these four might have given rise to warfare in the first place? Which of them continues to maintain it? Or has the anthropologist, impressed by a recurring cluster of traits in these three societies, overlooked the key factor which actually maintains warfare? To find out, more societies must be studied. The technique of using a few societies to demonstrate a point is much more useful in disproving a hypothesis by the careful analysis of a few negative examples studied in context than it is in providing support.

As an alternative to the laboratory that the anthropologist lacks, he occasionally selects, as S. F. Nadel (1952) or Fred Eggan (1954) did, the method of controlled comparison. He chooses societies that share a common set of conditions so that he can rule out the effect of these conditions upon one variable (that is, so he can "control" for them) while he studies the relationship of that variable to another. For example, if an anthropologist selected a set of societies that had certain characteristics in common such as their size, economic basis, and social and political structure, he would then be able to ignore or "control" these factors while pursuing his study of the relationship of a variable such as frequency of warfare to other variables such as the closeness of neighboring societies, the goals of warfare, or cultural values about making war.

This kind of procedure adds a measure of control, but once again it lacks the weight of numbers. Furthermore, it is often difficult to find societies which are matched for the desired set of variables.

Variations of the technique of controlled comparison have also been attempted in the field, where the investigator may either seek or create in the natural field situation conditions that enable him to control certain variables almost as well as he could if he used a laboratory. In fact, it has often been noted that certain types of anthropological investigations are "natural experiments." An example of this type of natural experiment would be studies of culture change, particularly of rapid and dramatic change, in which the conditions of change can be specified and the details of the process studied. One way to study such a topic is to find similar groups which are at various stages of culture change (say "Westernization") in order to compare the effect of some of the variables which are causing the change on certain other variables of interest. Thus a society in the remote Southern Highlands District of New Guinea which had only recently come into contact with Western culture might be compared to a similar but more Westernized society in the Eastern Highlands District in order to study the effects of the suppression of warfare on relations between groups, on female infanticide, or even on marital relationships.

Although this procedure by no means allows an investigator to control all of the important variables, it does offer him a favorable situation in which to attempt certain kinds of comparisons. Other natural experiments have occurred when whole communities were relocated, often with a change in their subsistence economy; relocations have been occasioned by such events as construction of dams, or, in one instance, as the result of the use of Bikini Atoll as a nuclear testing site. Recently, Michael Cole and his colleagues (1971) have called for the increased use of field experiments in anthropology, particularly in the study of psychological matters such as learning and remembering. Their own work in this regard is a promising innovation. For example, they found that the Kpelle of Liberia, who appear to be inferior to Europeans in mathematics and memory, can perform as well as Europeans or even better when the experiments used to test these skills are appropriate to Kpelle culture.

Another and more complicated form of controlled comparison was conducted among four East African societies by a team of anthropologists from the University of California, Los Angeles, headed by Walter Goldschmidt (1965). In each of the four East African societies that the project compared, part of the population lived primarily by farming in a mountainous region but another part lived by herding cattle on the arid plains below. The project attempted to determine whether this basic economic difference within each of four societies led to consistent differences in social institutions, values, attitudes, and personality dispositions. An anthropologist did fieldwork in each society, dividing his research between the farming and herding areas; a geographer visiting each research site systematically collected data on economic practices and potentials; and another anthropologist with psychological interests likewise visited each research site to interview and test large numbers of people. An example of one of their findings is the discovery that cattle-herders, who are historically more warlike, are also more independent and aggressive than farmers in the same society. The farmers, on the other hand, crowded together where quarrels can soon become a serious disruption to community life, try to avoid overt conflict and engage instead in indirect forms of aggression such as witchcraft (Edgerton, 1971).

A third strategy for cross-cultural comparison uses ethnographic data from a large number of published monographs. Applied correctly, this procedure can yield a valuable test of the anthropologist's hypotheses. The key, of course, is correct use; the large number of societies involved in the comparison usually requires the anthropologist to employ statistical procedures—various forms of sampling, choice of unit of analysis, operationalization, scoring, and testing the significance of the findings. Understanding these procedures and the reasons for them is essential for an appreciation of this kind of cross-cultural anthropology.

E. B. Tylor, an evolutionist and one of the founding fathers of anthropology, was the first to use statistical procedures for making a cross-cultural comparison. He applied them to the study of correlations, "adhesions" as he called them, between rules of postmarital residence and in-law avoidances. From such adhesions he attempted to reconstruct the ordered series of stages through which these societies were supposed to have evolved (1889). His efforts suffered somewhat both from the inferences he drew from his results and also from the limitations in the quality and the quantity of ethnographic data available at that time. Since the time of Tylor's study, nearly a century past, a much more accurate and extensive storehouse of descriptive materials on various cultures around the world has accumulated in libraries.

In the late 1930's, G. P. Murdock realized that as long as the information in these books lay unclassified and uncatalogued, it was most difficult for anthropologists to make effective cross-cultural comparisons using a large number of societies. Murdock set himself the goal of performing this task of classification and produced what is now called the Human Relations Area Files (HRAF). He used them himself to write his landmark book, *Social Structure* (1949), in which he correlated variations in the ways that societies classify their kin, with other variables of social structure such as rules of residence, rules of descent, and forms of marriage. He also attempted to identify which of the social-structure variables was most influential in setting off a chain reaction leading to a new classification of kin. This book was a monument to Murdock's method of comparison and it had a great impact upon cross-cultural comparison in anthropology.

The HRAF promoted extensive cross-cultural comparison from ethnographic sources. Anthropologists and students at the many universities that subscribe to the HRAF can easily and quickly obtain extensive information on some 267 societies under any of a great number of cross-referenced headings relating to a variety of social, cultural, economic, political, material, legal, or psychological matters. To look up the subject of warfare in the files, the anthropologist would look under the heading "Warfare" and would find all the relevant information taken from each society in the HRAF files. This information would be reproduced from the original monographs without modification; for some societies there might be 50 pages of

Under such major headings in the HRAF Catalogue as "War," "Instigation of War," "Wartime Adjustments," "Strategy," "Logistics," and "Tactics," there is a category called "Warfare" under which are listed the following sub-categories: wartime mobilization; departure of troops (e.g., public ceremonies, rituals for securing supernatural aid, exhortations to bravery); military expeditions (e.g., marching, scouts, protection of flanks and rear, camping, mounting of guards, foraging, billeting); types of combat (e.g., skirmishes, surprise attacks, assaults, pitched battles, siege operations); joining battle (e.g., choice of time and place, ritual preliminaries, and precautions); deploying and coordination of forces; special characteristics of naval and air encounters (e.g., duels between champions); termination of combat (e.g., after first casualty, after desperate last stand); tactical withdrawals; flight and pursuit; surrender; etc.

DATA FOR CROSS-CULTURAL COMPARISON. A description of resources in the Human Relations Area Files, from the HRAF catalogue.

information relevant to warfare, but for others there might be only a few. Based on this available information, the anthropologist would have to decide how to study such questions as: What are the tactics of war? Who participates in it? What are the consequences? And so on. He might look up subcategories in the files, such as ''Feuds,'' to see if additional information would be available there.

Following the plan of HRAF, Raoul Naroll (1970) developed a file that contains a random sample of societies for which there is high-quality ethnographic information. There are important reasons for wanting a random sample of societies. These reasons have to do with meeting statistical requirements, and they will be discussed further on. Naroll's file is called the Permanent Ethnographic Probability Sample (PEPS). Unlike HRAF, PEPS only cites the references for the subject in its catalogue. The user himself must then look up the references in the original ethnographic literature. One problem with PEPS is that many of these sources are not available in all the university libraries. In response to this problem, Douglas White (1970) has set up his Societal Research Archives System (SRAS) which, when completed, will become a computerized storage and retrieval archive for such information.

The Comparability and Standardization of Data

Anthropologists work and rework their materials when they write ethnographies, putting their data into forms they hope can be easily comprehended by fellow anthropologists. Consequently, each ethnography reflects not only the anthropologist's special interests, but the focus of the cultural pattern in the society he studied, as well as the diverse theoretical concerns of the field of anthropology at the time he made his study. And as the profiles of data in the HRAF indicate, anthropologists do not report on all aspects of culture equally well.

Cross-cultural comparison involves the anthropologist in a joint venture with the authors of ethnographic monographs who inadvertently become his "silent partners." The anthropologist, caught up in a particular problem, hopes that his "partners" have sought information on his problem and, even more important, have asked the kinds of questions he would have asked and collected the type of evidence that he requires. So difficult is it for any anthropologist to get others to approach a problem in precisely the same way and to gather comparable types of evidence, and yet so valuable is this kind of comparability, that numerous efforts throughout the history of anthropology have been aimed at standardizing the collection of ethnographic data.

As early as 1858, Lewis Henry Morgan, an evolutionist noted for his work on kinship systems, sent out questionnaires to missionaries and administrators living in societies all over the world. He collected valuable data on kinship systems but discovered, as have others who have used this method, that not everyone can be relied upon to respond rapidly or accurately. The more complicated the questionnaire, and the more peripheral its subject matter to the usual interests of the respondents in the field, the more difficult it is to persuade anyone to take precious time and effort making inquiries and filling in the requested data. But since many questionnaires are devised to collect data that are typically overlooked, the projects can prove valuable when they do succeed, though often pressures or inducements appear needed to gain cooperation. For example, Melville Herskovits succeeded in inducing about twenty anthropologists to spend perhaps a week of their time in the field collecting data on the perception of optical illusions. The results of the research led to a valuable book about cultural differences in perception, which included the finding that people who live in "carpentered" environments (containing right angles and straight lines), perceive the world differently from people who live in round houses or other environments that lack these carpentered features (Segall, Campbell, and Herskovits, 1966). However, for every success such as this one there have been many failures.

The anthropology student's training can instill basic techniques for collecting field data, and field manuals such as the Royal Anthropological Institute's *Notes and Queries on Anthropology* (1954) and Murdock's *Outline of Cultural Materials* (1950) can improve comparability where the classroom fails. However, the problem of standardizing all cultural data may never be solved for there are many ways to ask questions about the same thing and many questions which might be asked which are not at all obvious, arising only when a new problem is studied or an old question is asked in a fresh way. For instance, the anthropologist studying warfare might be interested in a possible connection between crowding and the occurrence of warfare. The work of Joseph Birdsell (1957), although based on a limited number of societies, indicates that long before a naturally expanding population has reached a situation of crowding, there is an expansion into new territory. However, if no land is available for expansion, or if available land is unsuitable for the population's economic pursuits, the society may develop other solutions. Among the solutions, which may include infanticide and contraception, is warfare. For a further instance, if the anthropologist wished to check his hypothesized relationship between "crowding" and the onset of warfare, he might want data not only on population size, which is usually available, but also on the ratio of population to carrying capacity of the land, a piece of information more difficult to obtain. The former item of information is fairly standard and easily measured. The latter is difficult to calculate, involving as it does measurement of variations in the food supply throughout the year, the amount of calories provided by all sources of food, the amount of calories needed to maintain the normal social and food-getting activities of the culture, variations of caloric intake according to age and size, and similar variables which are difficult to measure in the field and thus seldom found in ethnographies.

The ultimate expression of the desire to standardize data is the field comparison. In field comparisons, one anthropologist may attempt to collect similar data from a set of societies or from successive field trips to the same society, or a number of anthropologists who are members of a coordinated project may work in different societies to collect similar kinds of data. Just as the use of the HRAF for cross-cultural comparison is a substitute for experimentation in a laboratory, the field comparison is another way to obtain standardized measurement and a degree of experimental control.

These field comparisons may be loosely structured and coordinated, like the one sponsored by the United States Navy in Micronesia. In this instance, following the defeat of Japan in World War II, the Navy supported the ethnographic work of thirty-five anthropologists who attempted to collect similar kinds of ethnographic information in various parts of the Trust Territory of Micronesia (Foster, 1969). Other approaches have called for a team of anthropologists to carry out a coordinated comparison of several societies. For example, Alexander Leighton and his colleagues (1969) used the same procedures to study mental illness in various types of communities in Nova Scotia and later in Nigeria, being primarily concerned with the effects of social disorganization upon the amount and kind of mental illness in these societies; a team from the University of Chicago studied various social problems in six American Indian societies (Thompson, 1950), a Harvard team studied differences in values among five cultures in the American Southwest

(Vogt and Albert, 1966), and James B. Watson (1963) and a team of anthropologists from the University of Washington studied microevolution in four societies in the New Guinea Highlands.

Perhaps the best-known project of this sort is the *Six Cultures* study of socialization organized by Beatrice and John Whiting and their colleagues (B. Whiting, 1963). Six teams of fieldworkers were trained in the same data-collection techniques and then sent out to six quite different cultures to study differences in child-rearing procedures and to gather information on certain other variables such as household size, patterns of kinship, and mother's duties, which were believed to be related to differences in socialization. Despite these efforts to standardize, and a considerable expenditure of time and money, the interpretation of data from the project proved difficult because of the small number of societies studied. Clarification had to be sought by studying an additional 76 cultures taken from the ethnographic literature.

The conclusion for anthropology is clear. Because of the time and expense necessary to make even a small-scale field comparison, most cross-cultural comparison must be based on the ethnographic literature. Since the anthropologist interested in cross-cultural comparison cannot easily standardize the collection of field data, he must concentrate on standardizing his use of these data after they have been published in the ethnographic literature.

The Requirements of Statistical Analysis

The HRAF provided an invaluable service to anthropological investigators by making data from a large number of societies easily accessible. However, the existence of classification systems such as this does not mean that the problems and decisions are over for the anthropologist. Cross-cultural comparison is not an automatic procedure in which a data-collection mechanism scoops up evidence, passes it through a statistical formula, and drops an answer into waiting hands.

Choosing the proper statistical test for the job and meeting the requirements of this test may mean the difference between making an important contribution to understanding man's behavior and being led into a false conclusion. There are many examples of anthropologists whose "discovery" has turned out to be based upon a faulty use of statistics. Statistics is not as complex or forbidding a subject as its array of symbols would lead one to believe on first acquaintance. Neither is it a magic wand to be waved over data, causing an answer to appear. Any serious student of anthropology must become knowledgeable in statistics either by taking courses or by reading and learning from books such as Pelto's *Anthropological Research* (1970), Blalock's *Social Statistics* (1960), or Kerlinger's *Foundations of Behavioral Research* (1973).

The use of statistics enables an anthropologist to analyze a set of facts and arrive at certain kinds of conclusions about them. Statistical procedures can help him to make predictions about a culture he has not yet encountered from what he knows about cultures he has studied. He can sort out complex relations among a group of interacting variables. He can estimate the force that one variable exerts on another; and he can weigh the probability, if he finds that two variables are correlated in many societies, that his finding is significant rather than a chance occurrence.

It is important to understand how statistics help the anthropologist to carry out his comparative studies. For example, suppose that the anthropologist believes that war requires a certain level of political organization in order for a society to initiate and maintain hostilities. He feels that there must be a central authority to coordinate all the members of society so that while some fight, others provide food and other resources necessary to sustain warfare. He hypothesizes that war will occur in societies that have some form of central government and will not occur in societies that have no political organization that exists above the level of the bands which comprise them. He carries out his comparison in fifty societies selected to include twenty-five with central government and twenty-five without any form of government above the band. Suppose he finds that eighteen out of twenty-five of his central-government societies have warfare while only seven of the twenty-five band-government societies do. The results seem to support his hypothesis. But how strong is his support? To reach a decision, it is necessary to employ a statistical test of the *significance* of his results. Tests of significance permit him to determine how often the differences he found could have occurred simply by chance and consequently, how much confidence he should have in concluding that the relationship is not a chance one, but "real." If the finding in this example were submitted to analysis by the well-known chi-square test, it would be found that this result could be expected to occur by chance only about five times in one thousand, hence that the tested finding may be highly "significant"—that is, meaningful. Saying that a relationship between traits is statistically significant means that the probability is quite low that the traits under consideration would ever be found together in so many societies unless there was indeed a meaningful link between them. For example, we can conceive that in ten throws of two dice (each throw being an independent event) both dice might fall with ones up all ten times. Mathematical laws of probability have shown that the chances of this happening are very low indeed. The chances are so low in fact that if ten successive twos happened the skeptic might conclude that the events were not governed by chance at all, but rather by design, and he would check to see if the dice were loaded before placing any bets.

Since cross-cultural comparisons involve so any complexities, the investigator cannot expect to find a perfect correlation. In our example, where we correlate warfare with level of political organization, some of the societies with central government may be so corrupt or impoverished that they are incapable of warfare, while some bands may have interlocking networks of kinsmen who can be coordinated for purposes of mutual defense or retaliation. Because of factors like these, there will always be negative cases. Statistical tests are essential if the importance of negative versus positive cases is to be assessed.

The use of statistics is an advantage for the anthropologist, but his choice of societies and data must meet the requirements of the statistical test he chooses. Some tests, for example, require random sampling; others require certain kinds of data; most require that the units being compared be independent of one another. Each deviation from statistical requirements may distort conclusions; a serious deviation may invalidate them altogether. To avoid making damaging mistakes, the anthropologist has certain important and delicate decisions to make when tailoring the HRAF data or any other cultural data to the needs of a particular statistical procedure.

Finding Like Units

One requirement of all statistical comparisons is that the units which are being compared be alike. This might be termed the *"Grapes and Horses Problem"*: 8 grapes added to 8 horses would not give 16 of either item and it would be incorrect to attempt to add (subtract, divide, or multiply) them together. The units that the anthropologist deals with are usually "cultures" or "societies." Yet, some descriptions in the ethnographic literature are of bands, others are of tribes, towns, and nations. Are these the same kind of units? Consider for instance, the problem of correlating the presence of military organizations with the presence of warfare. A town which is part of a larger political unit may not be totally representative of the larger unit since it may lack, among other things, any military organizations of its own. Boys from the town may join a military unit and go off to war, but the town itself may nonetheless be rated as having no military organization. In this case, to use towns as units alongside nations and tribes as units would distort the anthropologist's conclusions.

Units are "alike" if they are defined by the anthropologist as similar in important ways (and not dissimilar in important ways). Which of the possible similarities the anthropologist selects as being important depends upon the problem he has chosen to study.

Galton's Problem

There is a second problem related to counting cultures or societies as units. This is known as *Galton's problem*—the problem of determining whether or not the units are independent. When two traits such as military organizations and warfare appear together again and again in a significant number of societies, the relationship between the two traits may be meaningful. If, however, military organizations and warfare occur together often because many of the societies once had a common origin or because they borrowed traits from each other, it could be a mistake for the investigator to count them as cases which have originated independently. He may actually be counting over and over again societies which are nothing more than duplicate copies of a few originals.

A glance at a map of culture areas of the world shows how traits may spread within an area either by the dominance of one original society or by culture contact such as that brought about by trade, marriage, or migration. As Driver and Schuessler (1967) point out, the incidence of traits being correlated may vary quite dramatically from one culture area to another. For example, bride price and patrilineal descent have a moderately strong worldwide correlation of .41 (of a possible 1.00) while in the Mediterranean area, the correlation rises to .60 and in North America it drops to only .03, or virtually no relationship at all. An anthropologist working exclusively in the Mediterranean might conclude that he had found a meaningful association; one with a knowledge of North American cultures could help him to see this association in perspective.

To take another example, suppose that the cross-cultural study of war leads to questions about the relationship of warlike behavior and sexual satisfaction—a scientific parallel to the slogan, "make love not war." One could hypothesize that people who permit premarital sex relations, multiple spouses, and adultery will be less likely to engage in warfare than people who permit none of these forms of sexual satisfaction. After operationalizing the terms and standardizing the units to be compared, suppose an investigator were to find that 37 of the 50 societies confirm the hypothesis—societies with "free" sexual behavior tend not to make war. It would appear that his hypothesis has received strong support. But what if he then discovers that 31 of these 37 societies were located in Africa? These 31 societies could conceivably represent 31 instances of a single original pattern, one that has rarely appeared elsewhere in the world.

Due largely to the work of Raoul Naroll (1970b), there are now various means for controlling Galton's Problem and, indeed, new cross-cultural files have been designed to contain only widely separated and presumably independent societies which have not been contaminated by contact with one another or by sharing a common historical background.

Sampling

The anthropologist has at hand only a slice of the total "universe" of cultures past, present, and future. And yet he often hopes that what he learns from the cultures he studies will apply to all cultures. If it is to apply, then the societies in his "sample," that is, the societies he selects to study, must serve as representatives for the rest of the societies, those he did not study. Therefore he hopes that his sample will be truly representative and that it will have all the characteristics of the societies contained in the "universe" and have them in the same proportions. If he draws a sample of societies to study warfare, he hopes that he has not drawn a disproportionate number of societies which have no warfare at all, because he is hoping to generalize his conclusions to all societies at all times and he wants to avoid reaching a misleading conclusion.

To avoid misleading conclusions and have a good chance of drawing a represent-ative sample, anthropologists often try to obtain a sample large enough so that all relevant characteristics have a chance of being included, yet one in which the items have been randomly selected. The first requirement of large size is usually easier for the anthropologist to fulfill than is the second one of random selection. For sampling to be random, all societies must have an equal chance of being drawn. The selection may be made random by a procedure as simple as drawing names out of a jar. It may also be made random by applying a table of random numbers; such tables contain lists of numbers arranged at random that can be used to select societies from a numbered list to make a sample.

For all societies to have an equal chance of being drawn, the total universe of societies must be known. But with cross-cultural comparison, it is impossible to specify the actual universe, since we know that many societies have never been described, and no one can say how many forgotten societies have existed on the earth in man's past. So when anthropologists today do cross-cultural comparison, they draw their samples not from any "true" universe of societies known in recent or past times, but from a file or catalogue of societies for which adequate ethnographic accounts are available. In this way an artificial universe has been created for statistical and sampling purposes.

When selection is random, bias from one society's selection may be matched by bias from another society in an opposite direction, and so the biases balance each other out in their effects. If the selection is not random, however, "systematic error"—bias in one certain direction—may creep in so that the sample is no longer a representative one, but is seriously distorted. For example, if a botanist wished to study the effect of sunlight and altitude on the shapes of the stems and leaves of flowers, and if he were to pick flowers only on the sunny slopes of a steep mountainside, those flowers would not be a representative sample of the total universe of flowers, which contains many flowers blooming only in shade or in lower elevations. Selecting a larger sample of sunny-slope flowers would only make matters worse, since the more flowers one picked on these sunny slopes, the greater the bias or systematic error in the sample. The same holds true for the anthropologist who is sampling societies. He will be better off with a small sample that is known to be free of bias or error than with a very large one which might contain systematic bias.

The societies in the HRAF are themselves a sample from the total universe of societies. If there is bias in the way anthropologists select their societies for study, then this bias is reflected in the files. One bias could arise from the fact that anthropologists have worked a great deal in some parts of the world and much less in others. In such a case, societies from certain culture areas would be overrep-resented, a problem which we mentioned when we discussed Galton's Problem.

The PEPS file consists of a randomly selected sample of societies which are well-reported. But if certain societies are well-reported because they possess characteristics that make them easier to study, there may be a bias in the PEPS file.

There are also other methods of sampling designed to help the anthropologist achieve a sample which is representative for the problem he wishes to solve. Early use of "haphazard sampling"—in which conveniently available societies were used without regard for their representativeness—has been replaced by a widespread form of sampling called "expert choice," in which an "expert" anthropologist reports that he regards his sample as representative, but does not provide any detailed explanation of how he reached that opinion. Despite the obvious inadequacies of this procedure, many of the best known cross-cultural surveys have sampled in this way. In "quota sampling," the anthropologist decides in advance what characteristics his sample should have, then finds societies to meet those criteria. For example, the investigator might decide he wants three societies from each of ten geographical areas, or four societies representing each of five economic types, or any twenty societies that have excellent information on witchcraft. In "probability sampling," all the societies in a universe are specified and then a procedure is followed which permits the investigator to state the exact probability for any particular society falling into his sample; perhaps he may wish to select every tenth society or every twentieth. "Random probability sampling," which we discussed earlier, is a special form of probability sampling that allows every society in the universe equal probability of occurrence in the sample.

For a large-scale study of warfare, the fact that societies influence one another could be a major factor in choosing items (societies or wars) to make up the sample for study. The warring societies may once have been members of the same group, or may have borrowed many of one another's social institutions—especially those of warfare, where each innovation must be matched, if possible. It is also true that warfare, like other aspects of culture, is guided by rules, and where societies have lived in close association over a long period of time, warfare can assume aspects of a shared combative ritual. The anthropologist may want to study this effect, and thus may choose a sample of neighboring societies, but for a study of other conditions affecting warfare, he may want a sample of independent societies. If he has developed a set of hypotheses about certain economic or political factors, he may use quota sampling to be certain that his sample includes representatives of all of the types of societies needed to test his hypothesis.

Probability sampling and random probability sampling are the ideal forms for the anthropologist doing cross-cultural comparison, but they are ideals which can usually only be approximated.

Coding the Data: Handling the Evidence

Once the anthropologist has specified his problem and drawn his sample of societies, he is ready to return to the meat of his problem—the evidence. Assessing the ethnographic evidence from diverse societies is a challenge to his creativity, ingenuity, and judgment, but there are a few general rules of procedure to guide him. The first important consideration is whether or not the relevant data can be found in the ethnographic literature. The anthropologist usually discovers that some data, such as those on socioeconomic organization, are easy to find. For example, if he were studying warfare, he might successfully gather information on kinship groups, forms of subsistence, types of military organizations, population size, area of land occupied, location of resources, and relations with neighboring groups. However, if he were interested in the carrying capacity of the land, in the long-term cycles which produce fluctuations in food production and population composition, or in the long-range versus the short-range effects of warfare, he would find the information more fragmentary if it were available at all. He might attempt to use his ingenuity to get indirect measures of some of these variables, or he might have to drop them from his consideration altogether with a request for other anthropologists to gather more data on such matters when next in the field.

Not all ethnographic information is of equal quality, and information from some societies is clearly more accurate than information from others. Raoul Naroll, who has devoted more attention to this problem than anyone else, has suggested (1962) that we should place our greatest confidence in fieldwork that was based, among other things, upon prolonged periods of firsthand research by a professional anthropologist who was able to speak the native language and attempted to do holistic fieldwork. These are useful safeguards, but the anthropologist might also wish to know something of the fieldworker's theoretical orientation, his training in methodology, and his emotional commitments and biases. The facts of an emotionally charged subject such as warfare might indeed suffer from prejudices both of the fieldworker who reports the information and of the anthropologist doing the cross-cultural study. It would be the anthropologist's responsibility to create a set of rules for sorting out accurate information from information which was less certain and for sorting out various inconsistencies in the evidence. He would have to keep the account of what actually happens in warfare separate from what the participants have claimed happens. He would also need to note the difference between the personal reasons which are given by participants for going to war and the additional factors which appear to precipitate action on a societal level.

The anthropologist engaged in cross-cultural comparison builds safeguards against confusions in the evidence when he operationalizes his concepts, thereby establishing rules and procedures for gathering this evidence. For example, a concept such as "crowding" might present problems for the anthropologist studying warfare. At the start of World War II, the Germans claimed to have gone to war over this concept, demanding *"Lebensraum,"* or room to live. What criteria should be used to measure "crowding?" Should the concept of "crowding" refer to productive capacity of the land, to spatial distance between living groups, to number of persons per square mile, or to each culture's own subjective definition of what constitutes "crowding?" At this point, the anthropologist's background knowledge, astuteness, and judgment must come to the fore in choosing which factors to use in his definition. Such questions as these show why it is important to operationalize so that everyone knows just how each concept relating to the evidence was defined. Every concept to be measured, including "war" itself, must be defined.

The anthropologist's next step is the actual "scoring" or counting of the presence or absence of the chosen factors which will become the body of his evidence. A *scoring manual* containing, for example, detailed rules for exactly how and when to count a concept as "absent," "present," or "strongly present" is usually made so that these procedures are as clear as possible. Since the investigator who made the hypotheses may be biased in favor of his own ideas, he should not do the scoring alone lest some of his judgments reflect his bias. Therefore several additional scorers, or "judges," are usually hired and trained to carry out the scoring process. It is important that these judges do their work independently of each other and in ignorance of the hypotheses that are being tested. In this way, they cannot be biased by each other or by a desire to prove or disprove the hypotheses.

The scoring process is crucial and it can become complicated. Let us assume, for example, that the investigator wishes to count the number of societies in which "crowding" is present, and let us assume further that he has clearly defined the concept "crowding" so that his scorers know how to recognize it. It is still necessary for these judges to assess the ethnographic evidence carefully before deciding whether or not crowding is present and if so, to what degree. For instance, an ethnographic report might indicate that a society had suffered severe food shortages during part of the time the anthropologist worked there. The judge would have to try to find out whether this situation of scarcity, which might indicate crowding, was usual for that society. If yes, he would have to decide how much scarcity there actually was and how to measure scarcity which varied over the annual cycle. If no, he would need to know whether he should score the society as having "crowding," "no crowding," "intermittent crowding," or something else.

As can be seen from the example, scoring the data can be a complex process. Obviously, then, a critical question to be answered is how well these independent judges agree with each other in their scoring. If their scores correlate highly it may be assumed that the traits in question have been defined clearly. Determining scorer reliability—the agreement between judges—is important. If the reliability is low it must be assumed the traits could not be measured reliably and that further analysis is consequently not worth pursuing; the concepts may have to be defined more clearly or abandoned altogether. But if the reliability is high, then the investigator can proceed with his analysis.

Analyzing the Data

The goal of scoring the ethnographic data is to translate descriptive materials from the sample societies into a form that can be properly counted and quantified.

This form enables the anthropologist to perform statistical operations on his data.

The computer revolution has supported the trend in anthropology toward large-scale analysis and cross-cultural comparison. It has enabled the anthropologist to use complex statistical procedures that can tell him a variety of things about his data. One type of analysis is a sort of "pattern analysis" that tells the investigator which of his variables are most closely associated. This pattern analysis is a version of the early evolutionists' concept of "adhesions"—variables that are closely related in a cultural pattern—but it is more precise and sophisticated in that it tells not only which variables are most closely related but also which are not, and also the strength of the relationship between them. A more usual type of analysis, however, is the search for correlations between specific variables. In the case of the study on warfare, the anthropologist might be seeking the correlation between warfare and military organizations, warfare and type of economy, warfare and degree of crowding, or warfare and population size.

Once the data have been tabulated and a statistical procedure applied to them, the anthropologist is in a position to discover whether or not his statistical results are significant—whether they seem to confirm his hypothesis, cast it in doubt, or reject it as highly unlikely. In strict statistical terms, to claim a significant result, the anthropologist must be able to reject the *null hypothesis*. The null hypothesis in statistics states that there is *no* significant relationship between two variables. Therefore a rejection of the null hypothesis is actually an affirmation of the anthropologist's hypothesis that there *is* a significant relationship between the two traits. This is a technical point, but an important one.

Let us say, hypothetically, that the anthropologist studying warfare made his correlations between warfare and the presence of military organizations and was able to reject the null hypothesis. He concludes that the two factors *are* significantly related. How should he interpret his finding? The point that we made before is an important one to remember here: a high correlation between two variables does not necessarily imply that a causal link exists between them. Neither does it indicate, if there is a causal link, which of the two "correlated" traits may have "caused" the other. Perhaps the presence of military organizations and the presence of warfare are both linked to a more basic cause such as crowding. Or perhaps warfare is the cause of military organizations which arise only after war has been initiated. Or the situation may be the reverse, namely that societies form military organizations—perhaps in imitation of their neighbors—and then come to use them merely because they exist. The reasoning in this latter instance would parallel the argument that the possession of nuclear bombs will lead inevitably to their use.

The anthropologist could take any of these positions, since there is nothing in the mere existence of a correlation that makes one possibility more likely than another. To make a decision about whether there is a probable causal relationship between two variables and if so, which variable causes the other, requires him to turn to other forms of evidence which bear on the question. An example of this kind of situation is the research which correlates smoking with heart disease. Some scientists believe that there is a causal relationship between the two, and that smoking is the cause of heart disease. Other scientists, however, reject the idea that smoking causes heart disease at all, pointing to the possibility that both smoking *and* heart disease are caused by a third factor, such as anxiety, which puts stress on the heart and at the same time encourages smoking as a means of calming down. Obviously, then, additional information must be collected and alternative hypotheses based upon this information must be tested if the question of causation is to be settled. There are also a number of statistical procedures which have been worked out which make it possible to infer from correlations both cause and the probable direction of the cause, but these procedures are complex, difficult to use, and somewhat disputed (Boudon, 1970).

We originally chose the example of a correlation between warfare and military organizations because it is an example of an important issue that we all know something about. In fact, however, actual studies of this correlation have been made. In general, these studies show that when military organizations exist, they will eventually engage in armed combat. This statement is true whether the organization is a small group of warriors or a huge standing army (Wright, 1942; Naroll, 1966). A more recent study clarifies this relationship. Anthropologist Keith Otterbein (1970) studied the evolution of war in 50 societies. Of these 50 societies, only 4 lacked military organizations and warfare and all 4 of these were located in isolated areas—islands, forests, or the arctic. Like Naroll and Wright, Otterbein finds that societies possessing military organizations go to war. He concludes that unless a society is so isolated from its neighbors that they pose no threat, it must have a military organization or it will be annihilated or absorbed (Otterbein, 1972).

What then is the cause of warfare? Is it the presence of military organizations? Is it the presence of neighboring societies which it is impossible to flee or avoid? Or is it conflict over resources? Or perhaps man himself? To answer these kinds of questions more information would be needed. What actually precipitates an armed clash? Is it a desire for revenge or a need for defense? Is it to gain plunder, tribute, or land? Is it to subjugate another society or merely to seek trophies and honors? (See Otterbein, 1972:92.) What conditions bring about the development of military organizations themselves? Do such organizations emerge because of conflicts over land, or hunting territory, or women? Until questions such as these can be answered, we must be satisfied with a partial answer to our basic question: Under what conditions does man make war on man?

Each attempt to present a hypothesis for confirmation and each attempt to put forth a causal explanation refer back to more general theories which anthropologists have about the nature of man and culture. To these more general theories anthropologists look for an understanding of man's cultural behavior, and it is these more general and often competing theories that the specific studies are attempting to support or challenge. As Thomas Kuhn has pointed out in his popular book *The Structure of Scientific Revolutions* (1962), scientific truth is in a continual state of re-examination and change. A hypothesis or a theory may be considered true until new hypotheses and theories emerge which explain the facts better and explain other facts in addition; thus what we consider to be true is modified. So it is with cross-cultural comparison. Such studies are interpreted by the best theories we have available, but always with the knowledge that these theories may be replaced when better studies are carried out.

Anthropology is a relatively young discipline, one that is still in a state of ferment—as are all the fields which take the study of man and his behavior as their domain. Theories that will lead to a better understanding of human behavior and culture can best be tested by methods of cross-cultural comparison. This task is therefore a fundamental one if anthropology is to progress as a science. Its success depends, however, on the quality of data gathered in fieldwork and the insight and accuracy with which the ethnographic information has been presented. In all these steps toward an understanding of culture, methods play a vital role and are influential in directing the course of anthropology. Knowledge of these methods is basic to an understanding of human behavior as it occurs in cultures throughout the world.

Further Readings

There are several general sources on explanation and comparison that will be useful to interested students. Pelto's *Anthropological Research* (1970) provides a somewhat more advanced discussion of both topics. A good introduction to explanation itself is provided by Abraham Kaplan, *The Conduct of Inquiry* (1964), and a very challenging appraisal of explanation in anthropology is available in A. R. Louch's *Explanation and Human Action* (1966).

A good overview of the problems and techniques of cross-cultural comparison is provided by F. W. Moore, *Readings in Cross-Cultural Methodology* (1961). The best available discussion of all the issues of cross-cultural comparison is Naroll and Cohen's *Handbook of Method in Cultural Anthropology* (1970). Unfortunately, the material in this book is intended for a sophisticated audience and will be unsuitable for beginning students.

One of the best ways to obtain a better understanding of the problems and procedures of cross-cultural comparison is to read books and articles that use this approach. A sample of such writing might include the following: W. Lambert, *et al.*, "Some Correlates of Beliefs in the Malevolence and Benevolence of Supernatural Beings" (1959); D. McClelland, *The Achieving Society* (1961); J. M. Roberts and B. J. Sutton-Smith, "Cross-Cultural Correlates of Games of Chance" (1966); W. N. Stephens, *The Oedipus Complex* (1962); Beatrice Whiting, *A Cross-Cultural Study of Sorcery and Social Control* (1950); John W. M. Whiting and Irvin L. Child, *Child Training and Personality* (1953); and F. Young, *Initiation Ceremonies* (1965).

CONCLUSION   ISSUES AND DILEMMAS

In a field of study as personal and human as anthropology, there are certain to be controversies. In the past few years, the image of anthropology itself has shifted. Until recently anthropology was typically seen as being the most liberal of sciences, the academic discipline most concerned with understanding and championing "primitive" peoples in out-of-the way places, or the poor and the ethnic minorities in our own society. Indeed, anthropologists have often been politically unwelcome because of their stubborn advocacy of the rights of others. Anthropology, at least since Boas, has been known by all for its steadfast insistence that all men are potentially equal, that all cultures deserve respect, and that human rights must be defended, *everywhere*. Anthropologists still hold these values and sometimes fight for them. But in the social and political turmoil that began in the mid 1960's, anthropology, like many sciences, has become embattled. Anthropologists today are unwelcome in various parts of the world, including parts of our own society.

The roots of this change are embedded in the rapidly changing events of our times. As students have demanded that universities set the pace in the search for rapid, even revolutionary social change at home, anthropologists have sometimes come to be seen as just another kind of academic person; too old, too much a part of the establishment. As ethnic minorities in the United States have continued their struggle for pride and for power, they have sought their leadership (and rightly so), not from anthropologists, but from within their own groups. In the process anthropologists have often become outsiders. Even American Indians, for whom anthropologists have so often served as political and legal advocates, from Lewis Henry Morgan right down to the present day, have sometimes condemned anthropology as a particularly objectionable form of paternalism and political do-nothingism. As political independence has come to countries that were formerly European colonies, anthropologists have become identified with the colonial past and with exploitation, rather than with freedom and progress. As United States military and intelligence operations have grown throughout the world, American anthropologists have been accused of clandestine activities on behalf of such agencies as the Department of Defense and the Central Intelligence Agency. Some

116

of these accusations have been motivated by political interests or simple ignorance, but in other instances, anthropologists have publicly accused some of their own colleagues of unethical involvement in clandestine military or intelligence operations. Several of these instances involving India, Peru, and particularly Thailand have been significant enough to receive widespread coverage by the press.

As a result of these and other developments, anthropologists have been re-examining the goals and ethics of their science. There has been an outpouring of debate, argument, and even bitter anger. As we write, there is no unanimity among anthropologists concerning the many practical, political, and ethical questions that have been raised. But the issues, at least, are much clearer than before, and they demand the attention of all anthropologists—and of all students of anthropology.

The first question is: Why undertake research at all? In a world so conspicuously marked by poverty, disease, racial conflict, warfare, and every form of human misery, how can anthropologists choose to engage in "research" rather than in direct social action to alleviate these scourges of mankind? Many students ask this question and condemn anthropologists for "ivory-tower" aloofness from mankind's plea for a better life.

This question has no simple answer that satisfies everyone in anthropology. The issues are too complex and too personal for that. Yet there is a basic position which most anthropologists share. Anthropologists are citizens too, and they believe in the value of direct social action. They are also scientists whose professional lives are devoted to providing a better understanding of man as a basis for more enlightened social action. Over its history, anthropology has made major scientific contributions to social action. For example, the concept of culture, in opposition to "racial" points of view, has produced essential evidence of the basic equality of mankind. That the most important human differences are a product of culture and not race is perhaps anthropology's most important contribution, one that has had a continuing impact upon the course of modern history. Other and specific kinds of anthropological research throughout the world have led to social change in political, economic, educational, medical, and other aspects of life.

Anthropologists who engage in basic research believe, as do other scientists, that even their most abstract and apparently nonrelevant research may someday prove to be of practical value for mankind. Thus, in the long run, theoretically significant research on color classification, primate social organization, or religious ritual may one day have greater importance for man than more narrowly focused practical research on poverty, disease, or conflict. Not all anthropologists justify their research on the grounds of its ultimate value for mankind. Some do fieldwork simply because they enjoy it, or because it relates to some theoretical interest of their own, or to achieve prominence. This point is important because anthropologists defend the right of the individual to choose his own research problems. This freedom is championed because no science can survive if the direction of its research is dictated primarily by social or political circumstances. If

POVERTY. (a) The slums of Rio de Janeiro (courtesy of Richard Wilkie). (b) Woman in Salta, Argentina (courtesy of Richard Wilkie). (c) Father and child in Guatemala (courtesy of Richard Wilkie). (d) Widow and children in Kenya (R. B. Edgerton).

C

D

it were, then anthropology would study racism one year, ecology the next, and who knows what after that? Liberal politicians would demand one kind of research while conservatives would demand another. Few anthropologists actually live in an ivory tower. They feel social and political pressures; all scientists do, even those whose research is apparently removed from immediate human concerns. But anthropologists are determined to build their science on scientific grounds, not on the demands of social action groups or politicians. The fundamental questions are these: What do we now know about man? What must we know next? How can we learn it?

In seeking, sincerely, the answers to these questions, a science like anthropology that is so directly concerned with mankind cannot fail to produce data that have both immediate and long-term importance for human welfare.

What right do anthropologists have to study other peoples? Anthropologists, with rare exceptions, are acutely sensitive to the privacy and dignity of other peoples. They study other peoples because of their conviction that the knowledge gained is essential to the welfare of mankind. This conviction is the ethical foundation of anthropology. Nevertheless, in some parts of the world, as among certain ethnic minorities in the United States, problems are raised; the people themselves ask, often in the most challenging terms, why they should be "studied." They demand social action, not "another study" in which they see themselves as "guinea pigs." They believe they know what their needs are and they do not want to be studied "to find out what we already know." Faced with such opposition, some anthropologists retreat. Others find ways, in team research with members of other disciplines, or alone, to give something of value in return for the right to live with a people and try to understand their culture; they attempt reciprocity. When confronted by angry members of a ghetto community the issues of reciprocity are crystal clear. But they are just as important when the proposed fieldwork involves a small band of so-called "primitive" people who do not understand what an anthropologist is, much less what he can do to help them or harm them. In both kinds of research, reciprocity is not only a practical issue, but an ethical one.

In the past, anthropologists went into the field with the conviction that they would do nothing to harm the people they studied and that they would help in any way they could. A maxim of anthropologists was to leave a community so that the next researcher would be welcome. And so they exchanged gifts and food, used their limited medical knowledge, gave their affection and companionship, and often tried to influence the government on behalf of "their people." There was something paternalistic in this arrangement and sometimes shocking mistakes were made, but there was also a kind of honesty in an arrangement that was based upon what people felt that they *wanted* to do for each other. Some anthropologists continue to operate in this highly personal way, giving and receiving as trust, emotion, and circumstance permit. We described earlier how Peggy Golde (1970) entered into the expected reciprocity system of the Mexican village she studied. Sometimes, however, it is not at all clear what reciprocity means in a culture. Laura Thompson's (1969:9) experiences in Fiji are a good illustration:

I had moved with the villagers to a temporary camp near their fishing grounds. One night a young girl was speared in the thigh by a swordfish. She was bleeding profusely and was expected to die. Upon the urgent request of the family, I treated her as best I could with the help of a Boy Scout manual. Fortunately, the wound healed. Failure would have meant a severe setback in the fieldwork. Soon, however, I noticed a change in the relations of the girl's family toward me. Semitchi, her father, began to ask many small favors: tobacco, some kava, trade goods, even my sunglasses, I asked a native the meaning of this behavior. Was I expected to pay the father for successfully treating his child, perhaps saving her life? "Oh," he replied, "that is natural. Semitchi assumes that you would not have bothered to treat his daughter if you had not thought that it would somehow work to your advantage."

Faced with moral uncertainties, other anthropologists are unwilling to begin fieldwork unless they are certain that they are giving as much to the people as they believe the people are giving to them. Such arrangements sometimes take the form of an informal or even written agreement.

Some anthropologists believe that merely establishing a reciprocal relationship is not enough. They insist that any anthropologist become an advocate for the people he studies. There is a growing sentiment among anthropologists favoring such advocacy, especially when the people are relatively powerless against local, national, or international economies or political forces. A dramatic example of this concern was the response of Filipino anthropologists to possible commercial exploitation of the Tasadays, a tiny band of stone-age people recently discovered in the forests of Mindanao. Working through Panamin (Presidential Arm for National Minorities), anthropologists found the Philippine government to be sympathetic to the defenselessness of the Tasadays against the encroachment of commercial logging. The result was that President Marcos set aside the Tasaday homeland as a 50,000-acre reserve to be free of outside interference.

Advocacy is hardly a new principle. Throughout history, anthropologists have devoted themselves to supporting the rights of people whom they were studying. Indeed, some anthropologists have specialized in research-advocacy of this sort, and a subfield of anthropology called "applied" or "action" anthropology has long been in existence. A good example is provided by a collaborative project between anthropologists from Cornell University and the Peruvian National Indian Institute. This experiment involved an effort to improve the quality of life of 1700 monolingual Indians who lived in slavelike serfdom on Hacienda Vicos about 250 miles north of Lima, Peru. Prior to the intervention of the anthropologists, these Indians were virtually without a voice in their own affairs and their standard of living was the lowest in the region. In 1951, the anthropologists leased the Hacienda for five years, taking responsibility for changing the lives of the Indians.

Their effort was to promote human dignity while learning more about human behavior in the process. They gave primary attention to changes in political and administrative institutions, health and education.

Initial results were remarkably positive, but when the anthropologists' lease expired and the Peruvian government was asked to buy the Hacienda and free the Indians, much political and economic resistance was encountered. In 1962, after five years of dispute and delay, the Indians' cooperative itself purchased the Hacienda. Cornell anthropologist Allan Holmberg, who directed the Project, concluded: "The major lesson of Vicos, for Peru as a whole, is that its serf and suppressed peasant population, once freed and given encouragement, technical assistance, and learning, can pull themselves up by their own bootstraps and become productive citizens of the nation" (Holmberg *et al.*, 1965:8). He concluded also that this experimental approach in anthropology, "may in the long run provide considerable payoff in terms both of more rational policy and better science" (1965:12).

There is little to quarrel with in the call for advocacy, when such direct help is clearly called for. Questions arise only when the demand for open advocacy is attached to all field research. In some instances, such a position would be politically impossible and would lead to the anthropologist's expulsion from the country in question. In other instances, the people themselves become advocates and that, too, can be dangerous. For example, Cora DuBois did fieldwork with the people of Atimelang on the Indonesian Island of Alor just before the Japanese invasion of World War II. Although DuBois had returned to America, several of her friends on Alor were heard by the Japanese to say that America would win the war. Five of these people were publicly decapitated as a warning to the populace (DuBois 1961:xiv). At about the same time, Rosalie Wax was doing fieldwork with the Japanese-American inmates of a relocation camp in the United States. Several of these people asked Wax not to interview them for fear that they would be thought stool pigeons and killed, as had happened to one of them earlier (Wax, 1971).

Another issue has to do with objectivity. If the anthropologist likes the people among whom he does fieldwork, and if he feels ethically bound to help them in every way he can, is it possible for him to maintain scientific objectivity? There is no simple answer to this question; each anthropologist must find his own way to balance his ethical conviction and his emotional involvement against his intellectual detachment. The methods and styles that this book introduces represent the ways in which anthropologists try to understand another people in what they hope is a fully humane, yet scientific search for truth.

As must have become apparent, there is no single, sovereign method or style in anthropology. There are many methods and many styles that are forever changing and falling into or out of favor among anthropologists. This state of methodological flux is as it should be. If there were one and only one method of doing fieldwork or one and only one style of presenting ethnographic data, then this method or style would become a tyrant dictating how the investigator must proceed. A carpenter whose only tool is a hammer can only hammer, he cannot saw. Methods are tools. These tools should not become ends in themselves to be pursued slavishly nor should they become so sanctified that they and they alone are thought to be acceptable. Sometimes methods and styles do tyrannize us—sometimes it is said that there is one and only one way to *do* fieldwork or only one acceptable way to present ethnographic information. Today, however, there is diversity, disagreement, and doubt about how one should best use methods and styles.

This state of affairs should not be seen as an indication that anthropology is not a science, or not *yet* a science. There is no scientific field that uses only one method. Percy Bridgman (1927), a Nobel Prize-winning physicist, put it as well as anyone when he said that all a scientist can do is use his mind and do his utmost.

A good anthropologist does his utmost to understand other people. He tries to be accurate, of course, and to leave nothing out, but whatever methods he uses, the heart of this understanding rests upon a shared humanity, sometimes referred to in the social sciences as *verstehen*. How powerful and elemental this capacity—and need—for understanding can be is illustrated by the life of Ishi, the last surviving Yahi Indian (T. Kroeber, 1961). Ishi entered the white man's world in 1911 when he staggered into a corral near Oroville, California. He was exhausted, terrified and starving. He was also the last surviving member of the Yahi, who formerly lived in the foothills of Mt. Lassen. By 1850 these Indians, like others around them, found their lands overrun by white men who farmed, ranched, and looked for gold. Many Indians were shot, others died of the new diseases these outsiders brought. The Yahi were able to hold out until 1911, because their land was so rough and remote, and because the Yahi hid every sign of their existence from the white men. For the last few years there were only four living Yahi, and when Ishi's mother died, he alone remained. For three years he lived completely alone. We do not know why he emerged when he did, but it had much to do with grief and loneliness. When the white men found him, he expected to be killed, for that was what Ishi knew white men to do to Indians. Instead, they took him to jail where news of his existence spread to anthropologists A. L. Kroeber and T. T. Waterman at the University of California, Berkeley. Waterman rushed to Oroville. No one, including several Indians from nearby tribes who were brought in to question him, knew Ishi's language. Waterman, who was a linguist, had word lists from a neighboring Indian tribe and he tried these words out on Ishi (T. Kroeber, 1961:6-7).

Ishi was attentive but unresponding until, discouragingly far down the list, Waterman said *siwini* which means yellow pine, at the same time tapping the pine framework of the cot on which they sat. Recognition lighted up the Indian's face. Waterman said the magic word again; Ishi repeated it after him, correcting his pronunciation, and for the next moments the two of them banged at the wood of the cot, telling each other over and over, *Siwini, siwini*!

With the difficult first sound recognition achieved, others followed. . . .Together he and Ishi tried out more and more words and phrases: they were beginning to communicate. After a while Ishi ventured to ask Waterman, *I ne ma Yahi*? ''Are you an Indian?'' Waterman answered that he was. The hunted look left Ishi's eyes—here was a friend. He knew as well as did his friend that Waterman was not an Indian. The question was a tentative and subtle way of reassuring and being reassured, not an easy thing to do when the meaningful shared sounds are few.

Ishi and Waterman had different reasons for wanting to understand one another but they shared a human joy when they did so. In the five years of life that Ishi was to have before tuberculosis killed him, he and Waterman and Kroeber became friends. They also came to understand one another, if only partially. Whether one achieves such an understanding with a single Indian or with an entire tribe does not matter. In either case the understanding is based on the shared humanity of all human beings. Anthropologists have developed methods that help them to achieve an understanding of different peoples and to convey this understanding to others. These methods and styles are important. They deserve to be studied and they need to be improved. But however useful they are, or may some day become, they can never be more than an extension, a sharpening, of man's human capacity to understand other men. Resting as it does on this human capacity, anthropology is and must remain a peculiarly human science.

GLOSSARY

affinal kin   Persons related by marriage.

age-grade   A social status based upon age, usually formalized by dress and responsibilities, and involved in a set of ceremonies and rituals.

anthropology   The science of man in the widest sense. Often divided into social or cultural anthropology, physical anthropology, archaeology, and linguistics.

artifact   Something made by man.

chi-square test   A statistical test which permits an evaluation of whether or not certain empirically observed frequencies differ from those which would have been expected under a certain set of theoretical assumptions.

clan   A unilineal descent group, either patrilineal or matrilineal, within which the specific genealogical connections with the founding ancestor are unknown so that many of the members are unable to say precisely how they are related to one another. The founding ancestor can be real, or imaginary (such as an animal or plant).

consanguineal kin   Persons related by blood.

controlled comparison   A kind of cross-cultural comparison in which societies are chosen for comparison because they possess or lack certain features which the investigator wishes to vary or hold constant.

correlation   The mutual relationship between two phenomena. In statistics, the correlation coefficient (Pearson's r) is the ratio of the covariation to the square root of the product of the variation in x and the variation in y.

cross-cultural comparison   The systematic comparison of various cultures in the search for generalized knowledge.

cultural code   The implicit rules for belief or behavior commonly understood by the majority of the members of any given group.

culture   There is no standard, commonly accepted definition. The most important criteria are that culture is shared behavior and ideas which are cumulative, systemic, symbolic, and are transmitted from generation to generation extragenetically.

culture shock   The psychological and emotional shock felt when one enters an unfamiliar culture.

depth interviewing   A type of interviewing that probes for underlying emotions, thoughts, and meanings.

125

diffusion   The process by which an item of culture spreads from one area to another. Essentially, borrowings by one culture from another.

divination   The process of foretelling the future or locating lost objects by various supernatural means.

ecology   The pattern of relations among organisms and their environment.

emic   Said of the meaning of something as it is perceived and understood by the participants in a culture rather than by the observers or outsiders.

energetics   A theory of human behavior and evolution based upon the ways in which people utilize the sources of energy in their environment.

ethnobotany   The study of how members of any specific culture classify and utilize the plant life in their environment.

ethnographic monograph   A book that attempts to describe the culture of a particular community of people.

ethnographic novel   A form of novel based upon people and events from another culture; conveys ethnographic details about the culture.

ethnography   The study of individual cultures; descriptive rather than theoretical.

ethnoscience   Basically, the system of beliefs and knowledge about the world and things held by groups of ''nonscientifically'' oriented people. The term is also used to refer to a method of ascertaining what these beliefs are.

etic   Said of the meaning of something as it is perceived and understood by an observer (outsider) rather than by the participants themselves.

event analysis   The detailed study of a single cultural event, often involving photographic or tape recording as well as other methods.

fieldwork   The anthropological method of research which involves prolonged residence in the community being studied.

functionalism   A theoretical position in anthropology that attempts to explain social or psychological phenomena in terms of the contribution they make to sociological or psychological well being.

Galton's problem   A problem, originally recognized by Francis Galton, growing from the fact that cultures may not be independent cases for analysis because of historical contact or borrowing.

genealogical method   A procedure for ascertaining patterns and behaviors associated with kinship through interviews in which an informant identifies persons related to him (consanguineal or affinal) by name and by the terms he and they reciprocally apply to each other. The inquirer, applying the resulting knowledge of kinship terms to observed behaviors, infers genealogy-associated expectations in the culture under study.

generalization   The process of inferring general principles or laws from particular instances.

Heisenberg principle of indetermination   A mathematical statement in quantum mechanics concerning the uncertain position of an observed particle in consequence of reactivity. It expresses the degree of uncertainty or indetermination in this position.

holism   The principle referring to the study of all aspects of a culture or a society in context rather than of a selected few without reference to their context.

humanism The branches of learning concerned with human thought and accomplishment as distinguished from science; examples include art, literature, history, philosophy.

hypothesis A proposition about certain phenomena that is capable of empirical verification.

ideal culture Beliefs, attitudes, or values about how people ought to "ideally" behave (as opposed to how people actually behave).

intersubjectivity Agreement between various observers upon the "facts" of a phenomenon being observed.

key informant A person who is willing and able to impart specialized or detailed information about his culture.

kinship Social ties based upon marriage, adoption, or blood relationship.

life history A type of interview that attempts to piece together an informant's life experiences in the context of his culture.

lineage A subsegment of a clan in which genealogical relationships can be traced to an actual person.

material culture Material objects manufactured as a part of a cultural tradition.

matrilineal descent Descent traced through the female line.

natural experiments A term referring to the study of natural conditions which, owing to some circumstance or event, can be examined in a manner similar to a laboratory experiment.

naturalism A research principle that directs the investigator to study behavior in the context in which it naturally takes place without disruption of the behavior or its context.

nuclear family The family composed of father, mother, and one or more children. It may be contrasted with the polygynous family or the extended family.

null hypothesis A proposition that states there is no relationship between certain phenomena.

observer bias Aspects of an observer's past experience that may cause him to observe behavior inaccurately.

operationalizing Stating the terms of one's hypothesis and research procedures in such a way that other investigators can clearly understand what was done, and can, if they choose, repeat the procedures themselves.

participant-observation A research method involving direct observation of a community's way of life and, insofar as possible, participation in it.

petroglyph Any drawing or incision on a rock made by prehistoric man.

projective tests Psychological tests which present to an informant such an ambiguous stimulus that whatever response he makes to it is more a property of his own experience—"projected" onto the stimulus—than it is of the stimulus itself.

rapport The relationship established between two or more people based upon common thought, interest, or sentiment. In anthropology, the relationship established between the fieldworker and the people he is working with.

reactivity   The effect an observer has on the phenomenon being observed.

role   The typical behavior associated with a status position.

sampling   A procedure by which a subset of a whole is selected in order to illustrate, exemplify, or represent that whole.

shaman   A widely found form of religious specialist who foretells the future, cures, and works various sorts of magic, often during dramatic performances or trancelike states.

sorcerer   A practitioner of magic usually intended to injure or control the behavior of others.

status   A position in a social system. For example, father, mother, banker, clerk, hunter, artist.

systematic observation   Formal rules and procedures for specifying what should be observed, when and how.

talking chief   A political leader who has achieved and maintained power or influence through his oratorical ability.

theory   An integrated body of general assumptions that purports to explain some given universe of behavior. For example, psychoanalytic theory, the theory of relativity. From a theory, one derives hypotheses which are capable of being empirically verified.

units of analysis   The specified phenomena which are thought to be sufficiently similar (in terms of some theoretical or conceptual assumption) that they can be categorized together and compared.

visual anthropology   The use of photographic techniques to study culture.

BIBLIOGRAPHY

Achebe, Chinua 1959 *Things Fall Apart*. Astor-Honor, New York.

Adair, Peter 1967 *The Holy Ghost People*. McGraw-Hill, New York.

Aginsky, B. W., and E. G. Aginsky 1971 *Deep Valley: The Pomo Indians of California*. Stein and Day, New York.

Bandelier, Adolph F. 1890 *The Delight Makers*.

Banton, M. 1957 *West African City*. Oxford University Press, London.

Barker, Roger G., ed. 1963 *The Stream of Behavior*. Appleton-Century-Crofts, New York.

Bates, Daisy 1938 *The Passing of the Aborigines*. John Murray, London.

Beals, Alan R. 1970 "Gopalpur, 1958-1960." In Spindler, ed., 1970.

Benedict, Ruth 1934 *Patterns of Culture*. Houghton Mifflin, Boston, 1934. Mentor, New York, reprinted 1946.

Birdsell, Joseph B. 1957 "Some Population Problems Involving Pleistocene Man." *Cold Spring Harbor Symposia on Quantitative Biology*, 22:47-68.

Blalock, H. M. 1960 *Social Statistics*. McGraw-Hill, New York.

Boas, Franz 1888 "The Central Eskimo." In *Sixth Annual Report of the Bureau of Ethnology, Smithsonian Institute*. Reprinted, Bison Book, with Introduction by Henry P. Collins, University of Nebraska Press, Lincoln, 1964.

Bock, Philip K. 1969 *Modern Cultural Anthropology: An Introduction*. Knopf, New York.

Bohannan, Laura ("Elenore Smith Bowen," pseudonym) 1954/1964 *Return to Laughter*. Doubleday, Natural History Press, New York; originally published 1954, reprinted with additions 1964.

Boudon, R. 1970 "A Method of Linear Causal Analysis—Dependence Analysis." In Naroll and Cohen, ed., 1970.

Bowen, Elenore Smith *Pseudonym: see Bohannan, Laura*.

Brace, C. Loring, G. R. Gamble, and J. T. Bond, ed. 1971 *Race and Intelligence*. Anthropological Studies No. 8, American Anthropological Association, Washington D.C.

Bridgman, Percy W. 1927 *The Logic of Modern Physics*. Macmillan, New York.

Briggs, Jean L. 1970 *Never in Anger: Portrait of an Eskimo Family*. Harvard University Press, Cambridge, Massachusetts.

Buck, Pearl S. 1931 *The Good Earth*. John Day, New York.

Bunzel, Ruth L. 1959 *Chichicastenango*. University of Washington Press, Seattle.

129

Capote, Truman   1965   *In Cold Blood*. Random House, New York.

Casagrande, Joseph B.   1960   *In the Company of Man: Twenty Portraits by Anthropologists*. Harper, New York.

Castaneda, Carlos   1968   *The Teachings of Don Juan: A Yaqui Way of Knowledge*. University of California Press, Berkeley.

   1971   *A Separate Reality*. Simon and Schuster, New York.

   1972   *Journey to Ixtlan*. Simon and Schuster, New York.

Chagnon, Napoleon A.   1968   *Yąnomamö: The Fierce People*. Holt, New York.

Codere, H.   1957   "Kwakiutl Society: Rank Without Class." *American Anthropologist*, 59:473-485.

Cole, Michael, J. Gay, J. A. Glick, and D. W. Sharp   1971   *The Cultural Context of Learning and Thinking: An Exploration in Experimental Anthropology*. Basic Books, New York.

Collier, J., Jr.   1967   *Visual Anthropology: Photography as a Research Method*. Holt, New York.

Conklin, H. C.   1955   "Hanunóo Color Categories." *Southwestern Journal of Anthropology*, 11:339-344.

Coon, Carleton   1932   *Flesh of the Wild Ox: A Riffian Chronicle of High Valleys and Long Rifles*. Morrow, New York.

Dark, Eleanor   1941   *The Timeless Land*. Macmillan, New York.

Dentan, Robert K.   1970   "Living and Working with the Semai." In Spindler, ed., 1970.

Diamond, Norma   1970   "Fieldwork in a Complex Society: Taiwan." In Spindler, ed., 1970.

Driver, H., and K. F. Schuessler   1967   "Correlational Analysis of Murdock's 1957 Ethnographic Sample." *American Anthropologist*, 69:322-352.

DuBois, Cora   1961   *The People of Alor: A Social-Psychological Study of an East Indian Island*. Harper Torchbooks, New York.

Edgerton, Robert B.   1971   *The Individual in Cultural Adaptation*. University of California Press, Berkeley.

Eggan, Fred   1954   "Social Anthropology and the Method of Controlled Comparison." *American Anthropologist*, 56:743-763.

Einstein, Albert   1953   "Geometry and Experience." In Herbert Feigl and May Brodbeck, ed., *Readings in the Philosophy of Science*. Appleton-Century-Crofts, New York.

Ekvall, Robert B.   1954   *Tents Against the Sky: A Novel of Tibet*. Victor Gollancz, London.

Eri, Vincent.   1970   *The Crocodile*. Jacaranda Press, Port Moresby, Papua New Guinea.

Evans-Pritchard, E. E.   1940   *The Nuer*. Oxford University Press, London.

   1954   *Social Anthropology*, Free Press, Glencoe.

Eysenck, H. J.   1971   "The IQ Argument: Race, Intelligence and Education." Library Press, New York.

Fernea, E. W.   1965   *Guests of the Sheik: An Ethnography of an Iraqi Village*. Doubleday, New York.

Filstead, W. J.   1970   *Qualitative Methodology: Firsthand Involvement with the Social World*. Markham, Chicago.

Firth, R.   1947   Introduction to Lin, 1947.

1957 *We the Tikopia*. Beacon Press, Boston.

Flaherty, Robert J. 1922 *Nanook of the North*. Film. Produced for Revillon Frères, New York.

Foster, G. M. 1969 *Applied Anthropology*. Little, Brown, Boston.

Frake, C. O. 1961 "The Diagnosis of Disease Among the Subanum of Mindanao." *American Anthropologist*, 63:115, 116, 124-125.

Freedman, M. 1968 Foreword to Margery Wolf, 1968.

Freilich, M., ed. 1970 *Marginal Natives: Anthropologists at Work*. Harper and Row, New York.

Freuchen, Peter 1931 *Eskimo*. Translated by Paul Maerker-Branden and Elsa Branden. Grosset and Dunlap, New York.

1961 *Book of the Eskimo*. Fawcett, Greenwich, Connecticut.

Gardner, R. G. 1964 *Dead Birds*. Film. Film Study Center, Peabody Museum, Harvard University, Cambridge, Massachusetts.

Gazaway, R. 1969 *The Longest Mile*. Doubleday, New York.

Geddes, W. R. 1957 *Nine Dayak Nights*. Oxford University Press, London.

Gide, André 1929 *Travels in the Congo*. Knopf, New York.

Gladwin, Thomas 1970 *East Is a Big Bird: Navigation and Logic in Pulawat Atoll*. Harvard University Press, Cambridge, Massachusetts.

Golde, Peggy 1970 "Odyssey of Encounter." In Peggy Golde, ed., 1970.

1970 (ed.) *Women in the Field*. Aldine, Chicago.

Goldschmidt, Walter 1969 *Kambuya's Cattle: The Legacy of an African Herdsman*. University of California Press, Berkeley.

1972 "An Ethnography of Encounters: A Methodology for the Enquiry into the Relation between the Individual and Society." *Current Anthropology*, 13:59-78.

Goldschmidt, Walter, *et al.* 1965 "Variation and Adaptability of Culture: A Symposium." *American Anthropologist*, 67:400-447.

Gould, R. A. 1969 *Yiwara: Foragers of the Australian Desert*. Scribner, New York.

Griffin, John Howard 1960 *Black Like Me*. Houghton Mifflin, Boston.

Gudschinsky, S. C. 1967 *How to Learn an Unwritten Language*. Holt, New York.

Gulliver, Philip H. 1966 *The Family Herds*, 2nd ed. Routledge and Kegan Paul, London.

Harris, Marvin 1964 *The Nature of Cultural Things*. Random House, New York.

1968 *The Rise of Anthropological Theory: A History of Theories of Culture*. Thomas Y. Crowell, New York.

Hart, C. W. M. 1970 "Fieldwork among the Tiwi, 1928-1929." In Spindler, ed., 1970.

Hays, H. R. 1958 *From Ape to Angel: An Informal History of Social Anthropology*. Knopf, New York.

Heider, Karl G., ed. 1972 *Films for Anthropological Teaching*, 5th ed. American Anthropological Association, Washington, D.C.

Hempel, C. G. 1959 "The Logic of Functional Analysis." In L. Gross, ed., *Symposium on Sociological Theory*. Row, Peterson, Evanston, Illinois.

Henry, F., and S. Saberwal, ed. 1969 *Stress and Response in Fieldwork*. Holt, New York.

Henry, Jules 1941 *Jungle People*. Vintage Books, New York, 1964.

Hogbin, Ian   1970   *The Island of Menstruating Men*. Chandler, New York.

Holmberg, Allan   1969   *Nomads of the Long Bow: The Sirionó of Eastern Bolivia*. Natural History Press, Garden City, New York.

Holmberg, Allan, *et al*.   1965   "The Vicos Case: Peasant Society in Transition." *American Behavioral Scientist*, 8:3-33.

Hospers, John   1960   "Implied Truths in Literature." *Journal of Aesthetics and Art Criticism*, XIX, No. 1, 37-46.

Houston, James   1971   *The White Dawn*. Harcourt, New York.

Huxley, Francis   1956   *Affable Savages: An Anthropologist Among the Urubu Indians of Brazil*. Viking, New York.

ImThurn, Everard F.   1883   *Among the Indians of Guiana: Being Sketches Chiefly Anthropologic from the Interior of British Guiana*. Kegan Paul, London.

Jenness, Diamond   1928   *The People of the Twilight*. Macmillan, New York.

Jensen, Arthur R.   1969   "How Much Can We Boost IQ and Scholarly Achievement?" *Harvard Educational Review*, 39:1-123.

Kaplan, Abraham   1964   *The Conduct of Inquiry*. Chandler, New York.

Keiser, A. L.   1969   *The Vice Lords: Warriors of the Streets*. Holt, New York.

Kerlinger, F. N.   1973   *Foundations of Behavioral Research*, 2nd ed. Holt, New York.

Kiki, Albert Maori   1968   *Kiki: Ten Thousand Years in a Lifetime*. Praeger, New York.

Kimball, Solon T., and James B. Watson, ed.   1972   *Crossing Cultural Boundaries: The Anthropological Experience*. Chandler, New York.

Kluckhohn, Clyde, and Dorothea Leighton   1946   *The Navaho*. American Museum of Natural History, New York, 1962 reprint.

Kluckhohn, Florence   1941   "The Participant Observer Technique in Small Communities." *American Journal of Sociology*, 46:331-43.

Kohl, J. G.   1860   *Kitchi-Gami: Wanderings Round Lake Superior*. Chapman and Hall, London.

Kroeber, Alfred L.   1922   Introduction to Elsie Clews Parsons, ed., 1922.

Kroeber, Theodora   1961   *Ishi in Two Worlds*. University of California Press, Berkeley.

Kuhn, Thomas S.   1962   *The Structure of Scientific Revolutions*. University of Chicago Press.

Kuhns, W., and R. Stanley   1968   *Exploring the Film*. Pflaum, Dayton, Ohio.

Kuper, Hilda   1965   *Bite of Hunger*. Harcourt, New York.

1970   *A Witch in My Heart: A Play Set in Swaziland in the 1930's*. Oxford University Press, London.

LaBarre, Weston   1969   *They Shall Take Up Serpents: Psychology of the Southern Snake-Handling Cult*. Schocken, New York.

LaFarge, Oliver   1929   *Laughing Boy*. Houghton Mifflin, Boston.

Lambert, W. W., Leigh Triandis, and Margery Wolf   1959   "Some Correlates of Beliefs in the Malevolence and Benevolence of Supernatural Beings." *Journal of Abnormal and Social Psychology*, 58:162-168.

Langness, L. L.   1965   *The Life History in Anthropological Science*. Holt, New York.

LaPiere, R.   1934   "Attitudes vs. Actions." *Social Forces*, 13:230-237.

Lawson, J. A.   1875   *Wanderings in the Interior of New Guinea*. Chapman and Hall, London.

Laye, C.   1959   *The African Child*. Collins/Fontana, London.

Leach, E. R.   1961   *Pul Eliya: A Village in Ceylon*. Cambridge University Press, New York.

Leighton, Alexander H.   1969   "A Comparative Study of Psychiatric Disorder in Nigeria and Rural North America." In S. Plog and R. B. Edgerton, ed., *Changing Perspectives in Mental Illness*, Holt, New York.

Levi-Strauss, Claude   1961   *A World on the Wane* (translation of *Tristes Tropiques*, Plon, Paris, 1955).

Lewis, Oscar   1951   *Life in a Mexican Village*. University of Illinois Press, Urbana.

1959   *Five Families*.   Basic Books, New York.

1961   *The Children of Sanchez: Autobiography of a Mexican Village*. Random House, New York.

1964   *Pedro Martinez: A Mexican Peasant and His Family*. Random House, New York.

Liebow. E.   1967   *Tally's Corner*. Little, Brown, Boston.

Lin Yueh-hwa   1947   *The Golden Wing: A Sociological Study of Chinese Familism*. Kegan Paul, London.

Linderman, Frank B.   1957   *Plenty-coups: Chief of the Crows*. University of Nebraska Press, Lincoln.

Louch, A. R.   1966   *Explanation and Human Action*. University of California Press, Berkeley.

Lowie, Robert H.   1935   *The Crow Indians*. Farrar and Rinehart, New York.

1937   *The History of Ethnological Theory*. Rinehart, New York.

1959   *Robert H. Lowie: Ethnologist*. University of California Press, Berkeley.

McClelland, D.   1961   *The Achieving Society*. Van Nostrand, Princeton, New Jersey.

Malinowski, Bronislaw   1922   *Argonauts of the Western Pacific*. Dutton, New York.

1929   *The Sexual Life of Savages in Northwestern Melanesia*. Routledge and Kegan Paul, London.

1967   *A Diary in the Strict Sense of the Word*. Harcourt, New York.

Marshall, J., and R. G. Gardner   1956   *The Hunters*. Film. Film Study Center, Peabody Museum, Harvard University, Cambridge, Massachusetts.

Matthiessen, Peter   1962   *Under the Mountain Wall*. Viking, New York.

1965   *At Play in the Fields of the Lord*. Random House, New York.

Maugham, Somerset   1969   *Ten Novels and Their Authors*. Penguin Books.

Maxwell, Gavin   1957   *People of the Reeds*. Harper, New York.

Mead, Margaret   1928   *Coming of Age in Samoa*. Morrow, New York.

1935   *Sex and Temperament in Three Primitive Societies*. Morrow, New York.

1970   "Fieldwork in the Pacific Islands, 1925-1967." In Peggy Golde, ed., 1970.

Mead, Margaret, and Gregory Bateson   1942   *Balinese Character: A Photographic Analysis*. New York Academy of Sciences.

Menen, A.   1948   *A Prevalence of Witches*. Scribner, New York.

Moore, F. W.   1961   *Readings in Cross-Cultural Methodology*. Human Relations Area Files, New Haven.

Moorehead, A.   1962   *The Blue Nile*. Harper, New York.

Morgan, L. H.   1870   *Systems of Consanguinity and Affinity of the Human Family*. Smithsonian Institution, Washington, D.C.

Mowat, Farley   1952   *People of the Deer*. Little, Brown, New York.

Murdock, G. P.   1949   *Social Structure*. Macmillan, New York.

1950   *Outline of Cultural Materials*. Human Relations Area Files, New Haven.

Nabokov, Peter   1967   *Two Leggings: The Making of a Crow Warrior*. Thomas Y. Crowell, New York.

Nadel, S. F.   1942   *A Black Byzantium*. Oxford University Press, London.

1952   "Witchcraft in Four African Societies: An Essay in Comparison." *American Anthropologist*, 54:18-29.

Nader, Laura   1970   "From Anguish to Exultation." In Peggy Golde, ed., 1970.

Naroll, Raoul   1962   *Data Quality Control: A New Research Technique*. Free Press, Glencoe, Illinois.

1966   "Does Military Deterence Deter?" *Trans-action*, 3:14-20.

1970a   "Cross-Cultural Sampling." In Naroll and Cohen, ed., 1970.

1970b   "Galton's Problem." In Naroll and Cohen, ed., 1970.

Naroll, Raoul, and Ronald Cohen, ed.   1970   *Handbook of Method in Cultural Anthropology*. Natural History Press, Garden City, New York.

Nash, D.   1963   "The Ethnologist as Stranger: An Essay in the Sociology of Knowledge." *Southwestern Journal of Anthropology*, 19:149-167.

Nash, D., and R. Wintrob   1972   "The Emergence of Self-Consciousness in Ethnography." *Current Anthropology*, 13:5: 527-542.

Niggli, Josephina   1945   *Mexican Village*. University of North Carolina Press, Chapel Hill.

Opler, M.   1965   *An Apache Life Way*. Cooper Square Publishers, New York.

Oswalt, Wendell H.   1973   *Habitat and Technology: The Evolution of Hunting*. Holt, New York.

Otterbein, Keith F.   1972   *Comparative Cultural Analysis: An Introduction to Anthropology*. Holt, New York.

1970   *The Evolution of War: A Cross-Cultural Study*. Human Relations Area Files, New Haven.

Parsons, Elsie Clews, ed.   1922   *American Indian Life*. Huebsch, New York.

Pelto, P. J.   1970   *Anthropological Research: The Structure of Inquiry*. Harper, New York.

Poncins, Gontran de   1941   *Kabloona*. Bantam Books, New York.

Powdermaker, Hortense   1966   *Stranger and Friend: The Way of An Anthropologist*. Norton, New York.

Prescott, P. S.   1971   Review of Houston, 1971. *Newsweek*, April 26, 1971.

Radcliffe-Brown, A. R.   1948   *The Andaman Islanders*. Free Press, Glencoe, Illinois.

Radin, Paul   1926   *Crashing Thunder: The Autobiography of a Winnebago Indian*. Appleton, New York.

1927a   *Primitive Man as Philosopher*. Appleton, New York.

1927b   *The Story of the American Indian*. Liveright Publishing Corporation, New York.

Rasmussen, Knud   1908   *The People of the Polar North: A Record*. Kegan Paul, London.

Read, K. E.   1965   *The High Valley*. Scribner, New York.

Reeve, C.   1785   *The Progress of Romance & The History of Charoba, Queen of Egypt*. The Facsimile Text Society, New York, 1930. (Reproduced from Colchester Edition, 1785).

Richardson, S. A., B. S. Dohrenwend, and D. Klein   1965   *Interviewing: Its Forms and Functions*. Basic Books, New York.

Riesman, David   1964   Foreword, to Elenore Smith Bowen/Laura Bohannan, *Return to Laughter*. Doubleday, Natural History Library, New York.

Ritzenthaler, Pat   1966   *The Fon of Bafut*. Thomas Y. Crowell, New York

Robbins, M.   1966   "Material Culture and Cognition." *American Anthropologist*, 68:745-748.

Roberts, J. M., and B. J. Sutton-Smith   1966   "Cross-Cultural Correlates of Games of Chance." *Behavior Science Notes*, 1:134-144.

Royal Anthropological Institute of Great Britain and Ireland.   1954   *Notes and Queries on Anthropology*, 6th ed. Routledge and Kegan Paul, London.

Sartre, Jean-Paul   1970   "Jean Paul Sartre: An Interview." *New York Review of Books*, Vol. XIV, No. 6, March 26, 1970, pp. 22-31.

Schneebaum, Tobias   1969   *Keep the River on Your Right*. Grove Press, New York.

Schusky, E. L.   1965   *Manual for Kinship Analysis*. Holt, New York.

Segall, M., D. Campbell, and Melville J. Herskovits   1966   *The Influence of Culture on Visual Perception*. Bobbs-Merrill, Indianapolis, Indiana.

Simmons, L. W.   1942   *Sun Chief: The Autobiography of a Hopi Indian*. Yale University Press, London.

Snow, C. P.   1959   *The Two Cultures and the Scientific Revolution*. Cambridge University Press, London.

Spindler, G. D., ed.   1970   *Being an Anthropologist: Fieldwork in Eleven Cultures*. Holt, New York.

Stands-in-Timber, J. and M. Liberty   1967   *Cheyenne Memories*. University of Nebraska Press, Lincoln.

Stephens, W. N.   1962   *The Oedipus Complex*. Free Press, Glencoe, Illinois.

Sugihara, Y., and D. Plath   1969   *Sensei and his People: The Building of a Japanese Commune*. University of California Press, Berkeley.

Sullivan, M. A., S. A. Queen, and R. C. Patrick, Jr.   1958   "Participant Observation as Employed in the Study of a Military Training Program." *American Sociological Review*, 23:660-667.

Thesiger, W.   1964   *The Marsh Arabs*. Penguin Books.

Thomas, Elizabeth Marshall   1959   *The Harmless People*. Knopf, New York.

Thompson, Laura   1950   "Action Research Among American Indians." *Scientific Monthly*, 70:34-40.

1969   *The Secret of Culture*. Random House, New York.

Tindale, Norman   1937   "Sub-incision." Reel 7 of Warburton Range Expedition of 1935. Film. Board for Anthropological Research, University of Adelaide.

Tomkievicz, S.   1971   "Flaubert and Madam Bovary." *Horizon*, Vol. XIII, No. 1, pp. 114-119.

Turnbull, Colin   1961   *The Forest People: A Study of the Pygmies of the Congo*. Simon and Schuster, New York.

1965   *Wayward Servants*. Simon and Schuster, New York.

1972   *The Mountain People*. Simon and Schuster, New York.

Turner, Victor W.   1957   *Schism and Continuity in an African Society*. Manchester University Press.

Tylor, Edward Burnett   1889   "On a Method of Investigating the Development of

Institutions Applied to the Laws of Marriage and Descent." *Journal of the Royal Anthropological Institute*, 18:245-269.

Underhill, Ruth   1940   *Hawk over Whirlpools*. J. J. Augustin Publishers, New York.

Vogt, E., and E. M. Albert, ed.   1966   *The People of Rimrock: A Study of Values in Five Cultures*. Harvard University Press, Cambridge, Massachusetts.

Watson, James B.   1963   "A Micro-Evolution Study in New Guinea." *Journal of the Polynesian Society*, 72:188-192.

Wax. Rosalie   1971   *Doing Fieldwork, Warnings and Advice*. University of Chicago Press.

Webb, E. J., D. T. Campbell, R. D. Schwartz, and L. Sechrest   1966   *Unobtrusive Measures: Non-reactive Research in the Social Sciences*. Rand McNally, Chicago.

Wells, A. E.   1971   *Men of the Honey Bee*. Rigby, Sydney.

Weltfish, Gene   1965   *The Lost Universe*. Ballantine Books, New York.

West, Morris   1957   *Children of the Shadows*. Morrow, New York.

White, Douglas R.   1970   "Societal Research Archives System: Retrieval, Quality Control and Analysis of Comparative Data." In Naroll and Cohen, ed., 1970.

Whiting, Beatrice   1950   *A Cross-Cultural Study of Sorcery and Social Control in Paiute Society*. Viking Fund Publications in Anthropology, No. 15.

1963   *Six Cultures: Studies of Child Rearing*. Wiley, New York.

Whiting, Beatrice, and John M. W. Whiting   1970   "Methods for Observing and Recording Behavior." In Naroll and Cohen, ed., 1970.

Whiting, John M. W., and Irvin L. Child   1953   *Child Training and Personality: A Cross-Cultural Study*. Yale University Press, New Haven and London.

Whiting, John M. W., Irvin L. Child, W. W. Lambert, and associates   1968   *Field Guide for the Study of Socialization*. Wiley, New York.

Williams, Thomas R.   1967   *Field Methods in the Study of Culture*. Holt, New York.

Wilson, Edmund   1956   *A Piece of My Mind*. Farrar, Straus and Cudahy, New York.

Winter, Edward H.   1959   *Beyond the Mountains of the Moon. The Lives of Four Africans*. University of Illinois Press, Urbana.

Wiser, William, and Charlotte Wiser   1969   *Behind Mud Walls 1930-1960*. University of California Press, Berkeley.

Wolf, Eric R.   1964   *Anthropology*. Prentice-Hall, Englewood Cliffs, New Jersey.

Wolf, Margery   1968   *The House of Lim: A Study of a Chinese Farm Family*. Appleton-Century-Crofts, New York.

Wright, Quincy   1942   *A Study of War*. University of Chicago Press.

Yoors, J.   1967   *The Gypsies*. Simon & Schuster, New York.

Young, F.   1965   *Initiation Ceremonies: A Cross-Cultural Study of Status Dramatization*. Bobbs-Merrill, New York.

Zelditch, M., Jr.   1962   "Some Methodological Problems of Field Studies." *American Journal of Sociology*, 67:566-76.

AUTHOR INDEX

137

SUBJECT INDEX